SUCCESSFUL
SPOUSE SELECTION

To Clintone

From Mrs. Banks
2/20/2018

SUCCESSFUL
SPOUSE SELECTION

T. L. ROGERS

Scripture taken from the HOLY BIBLE, NEW INTERNATIONAL VERSION ®. Copyright © 1973, 1978, 1984 by International Bible Society. Used by permission of Zondervan Publishing House.

The "NIV" and "New International Version" trademarks are registered in the United States Patent and Trademark Office by International Bible Society. Use of either trademark requires the permission of International Bible Society.

This book was printed in the United States of America.

To order additional copies of this book, contact:
Xlibris Corporation
1-888-795-4274
www.Xlibris.com
Orders@Xlibris.com
25077

CONTENTS

INTRODUCTION

Spouse Selection—What's It All About?

If there is one decision in life that requires a great amount of certainty, it is the choice of a wife or husband—the person with whom you will spend the rest of your life. For Christians, it is the second most important decision you will make in your lifetime; the first is allowing Jesus Christ to be the Lord and Savior of your life. You can change your job, change your automobile, change your residence—even change your name—without damaging your life or the lives of those around you; but this is not the case with marriage. The proper choice of a spouse can be either a blessing or a curse.

Some would argue that getting married or not, or whom to marry, are really not life altering decisions. These individuals think when something is broken, even a marriage, you simply replace it rather than fix it. They believe that a bad marriage can be easily undone, after all marriages are undone every day in courts across America. After the "transaction" is complete and you are legally divorced, you simply count your losses and move on. But that is a shallow view of a terribly life-altering decision.

The fact is that though the legal bonds of marriage can be undone by divorce, the emotional bonds are much harder to break. Divorcing a mate is not a painless, trouble-free event. For, you are attempting to unravel a multi-dimensional and complicated relationship. When you unite in holy matrimony, you are fusing with your spouse—literally forming emotional and physical bonds. You become joined to that person in your spirit as well as in your flesh.

When a husband and wife divorce, they must attempt to sever an emotional bond that is not so easily broken. It is a spiritual as well as a familial bond—one that overlooks faults and short-comings, links two families, triumphs with victories, laments during hard times, and provides companionship. All these things are what made the marriage work . . . at least for a time. But now you've grown apart. You say you're not in love anymore. You're sick of each other, angry and disappointed. Wake up! These feelings do not destroy a bond that was cemented by love. Love is a decision, not a feeling.

Consider this commonplace example: A few years ago, I wanted to change the location of my office. In order to do so, I had to dismantle bookcases that had been custom-built. At the time they were being constructed, I remember the carpenter using something called "liquid nails" to adhere the wood. Obviously, we assumed that the bookcases would be in my office forever—a permanent fixture. But after six years of satisfaction, dissatisfaction set in and my opinion of the bookcases changed when I decided to move my study to more spacious quarters. So I proceeded to dismantle the exquisitely constructed bookcases. But to my surprise, the bookcases did not "want" to be dismantled. In fact, as I attempted to force this "break up," the wood split inches from the joints and seams, rendering it useless for all practical purposes. The point is that the liquid nails had created such a strong bond that the bookcases could not be dismantled without tearing and ripping the wood apart. Perhaps (in a similar but more serious way) you have changed your mind about your marriage. The marriage and spouse that previously brought you so much satisfaction and joy have now become a source of agony and duress. Or maybe you simply want a change in venue. However, the attachment of your heart to your spouse's heart has not changed. Divorces try to dismantle relationships neatly and gently; but history demonstrates that, in order to do this, both parties will inevitably be torn apart. In other words, you can move away from each other physically, but your hearts will still be attached. In many respects your spouse has become you and you have become your spouse. In this process you are really attempting to leave yourself. For most, this is a heart-wrenching experience.

One divorced and remarried friend described the experience this way:

> *Divorce is so much worse than losing a spouse through death. When the death of a spouse occurs, as difficult as it may be, it is easier to release that individual emotionally because the loss can be grieved and afterwards one*

can move forward with life. This is primarily because there are no longer physical and visual encounters with that individual.

On the other hand, divorcing a spouse from whom there has only been physical separation (i.e., out of the same residence) contact inevitably still continues. It is like trying to get rid of a corpse that never really goes away. The individual is always around, particularly if children were born from that union. Constant interaction with the other parent is unavoidable. There's Christmas; children's birthdays—not to mention graduations and other special events. Perhaps even more significant is the shared visiting times with the ex-spouse. The interactions can continue for a lifetime.

For the single person observing all this from a distance, the conclusion is one of dismay. The same is true of those who are contemplating remarriage after having already experienced divorce. That is why the choice of a life partner is (for most people) a frightening, risky, and sometimes "tricky" endeavor.

With all of the above in mind, let us consider the legitimate concerns and questions that most single people have concerning marriage. They include the following questions:

Will the person that I marry . . .

> Love me for a lifetime?
> Be faithful to me for a lifetime?
> Make a good parent?
> Misuse our finances?
> Clash in personality with me?
> Be open and honest with me about the past?
> Have hidden secrets that will surface to destroy our marriage?

The risks and uncertainties of selecting a spouse in our society are evidenced by three key statistics:

1. 670 marriages out of every 1000 end in divorce.
2. Fewer people are getting married and, when they do, they are getting married much later in life than was the case three decades ago.

3. An increasing number of couples are opting for a "non-marital" union. They choose to move in together and just "play house."

Selecting a lifelong spouse for a happy and successful marriage need not be a game of Russian roulette, with the result being a failed marriage and another divorce statistic. It can and should be a wonderful and rewarding experience. And, while marriage is certainly a challenging pursuit, there are certain guidelines that can assist you when choosing a spouse. However, what is equally, if not more important than choosing a good spouse is being a good candidate for spousal selection yourself.

CHAPTER 1

Before You Start Looking

Successful Spouse Selection begins with *being* a successful person. And, in order to make a successful selection and be in a successful relationship, you must first have a strong relationship with God.

> *But if we walk in the light, as he is in the light, we have fellowship with one another, and the blood of Jesus, his Son, purifies us from all sin.*
>
> (1 John 1:7)

John suggests a truth that is important for developing and maintaining healthy, vibrant, and long-lasting relationships. In this verse, he presents a principle for relationships that is transferable anywhere. Through the aid of the Holy Spirit, he contends that if we are walking in the light (that is, the light of God's word, the light of His love, the light of His Spirit), we will have fellowship with one another.

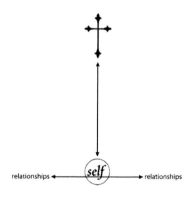

The foundation and genesis for a great human relationship is a great spiritual relationship with God. This suggests that if our relationship with God (vertical) is what it ought to be, then our relationships with our friends, family, children, and spouse (horizontal) will likewise be as they ought to be. Conversely, if our relationship with God is out of line—if we are not on good speaking terms with our Heavenly Father—we will certainly have trouble in our earthly relationships.

I believe that when two individuals are at odds in their relationship, the problem is not really about *their* relationship with each other but with their relationship (or lack of relationship) with God. If I begin to ask about their daily quiet time, commitment to Bible study, regular church attendance, family devotions, and prayer between husband and wife, the fracture between the individual and God will soon become apparent. This bears repeating! People who are not getting along with God won't get along very well with others.

The following illustration portrays the connection that our everyday relationships have with our relationship with the Heavenly Father. The illustration is of three circles that represent the totality of our lives. Each circle is filled with the many things that consume our lives on a daily basis (i.e., family, job, money, stress, music, education, entertainment, sexuality). Each dot in the circle represents one of those things.

Circle One

The first circle represents the person without Christ in his or her life.

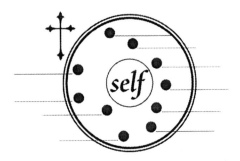

The man without the Spirit does not accept the things that come from the Spirit of God, for they are foolishness to him, and he cannot understand them, because they are spiritually discerned.

(1 Corinthians 2:14)

In this circle, self is seated on the throne of the individual's life. Basically, this individual operates from the premise of "I do what I want to do." Because self is on the throne, self dictates what is done with all the things in the person's life. If you asked someone like this the questions below, they probably would respond in the following manner:

Q: Who controls your money?
A: I do what I want to do.
Q: Who controls your time?
A: I do what I want to do.
Q: Who determines the relationships you maintain with your family and friends?
A: I do what I want to do.
Q: What about your choice of music?
A: I do . . .
Q: What about your choice of school?
A: I do . . .
Q: What about your sexuality?
A: I do . . .

Notice that for this particular individual, Christ is on the outside of the circle of his or her life. Self controls and manipulates every action and reaction. The scripture tells us that these people consider the biblical and spiritual principles unnecessary or, even, absurd. It is really a waste of your time to talk to these people about regular church attendance and Bible study. Don't even consider mentioning the virtues of moral purity and abstinence. More often than not, they will laugh at your spiritual suggestions because ". . . they are foolishness to him." (1 Corinthians 2:14)

Circle Two

The second circle represents the Immature Christian.

Brothers, I could not address you as spiritual but as worldly—mere infants in Christ. I gave you milk, not solid food, for you were not yet ready for it. Indeed, you are still not ready. You are still worldly. For since there is jealousy and quarreling among you, are you not worldly? Are you not acting like mere men? For when one says, "I follow Paul," and another, "I follow Apollos, are you not mere men?"

(1 Corinthians 3:1-4)

This circle resembles the first circle, but there are a few important differences. All the things that were in the life of the person in Circle One remain in Circle Two. The individual continues to be under the dominance and control of self. However, there is a fundamental difference between the man or woman of Circle One and the individual in Circle Two. The person in Circle Two has been born again.

Closely observe the text again. To describe the person, the writer used the phrase ". . . in Christ." In other words, this person has genuinely been born into the family of God, commonly referred to as being "born again." But note that the reference is to an infant. This reference helps us understand the contrast to the individual in Circle One who has not been born again. It is interesting that Paul uses the term "infant." The term is appropriate because babies can make dreadful mistakes. These mistakes are generally overlooked by parents because it is normal for a baby to be immature. Certainly, babies will make mistakes that adults will not make. When an infant wets, stumbles when trying to walk, or dribbles when eating, we overlook these occurrences and consider them quite normal. But if at the age of 12 that same child exhibits these infant-like behaviors, we begin to suspect that he or she has some developmental problems.

There are many Christians who are in this circle-infant-like in terms of their level of spiritual maturity. There is actual longevity in their faith walk, yet they are still quite immature. The only difference in the two circles is that Christ is inside Circle Two. But he is only one of many things inside the circle. The reason for the state of immaturity is that while Christ is in the immature Christian's life, He does not hold the place of prominence—center circle—which is needed for maturity.

If you ask the same series of questions to this person, you will get the same general responses that you received from the person in Circle One.

Q: Who controls your money?

A: I do what I want to do.

Q: Who controls your time?

A: I do what I want to do.

Q: Who determines the relationships you maintain with your family and friends?

A: I do what I want to do.

Q: What about your choice of music?

A: I do . . .

Q: What about your choice of school?

A: I do . . .

Q: What about your sexuality?

A: I do . . .

Sadly, most churches in America are filled with people who are in Circle Two. That explains why sinful acts are so prevalent in the church today. You cannot expect this person to be available for Bible study, to serve in ministry, or to give a tithe of their income to the work of God's house. At best, you can expect him or her to be a good Sunday morning pew-warmer.

Don't forget our initial premise: the person who is not in a right relationship with God will struggle in all other relationships. When persons who confess to be Christians have themselves seated at the controls of their lives, their lives will be just as chaotic as the non-believer's. But there is one last circle.

Circle Three

The third circle represents the Spiritually Mature Christian.

The spiritual man makes judgments about all things, but he himself is not subject to anyone's judgment: "For who has known the mind of the Lord that he may instruct him?" But we have the mind of Christ.

(I Corinthians 2:15-16)

Notice the obvious changes that have occurred in this circle. There is order in this person's life. The challenging issues that confront him or her have not changed or diminished. Notice that the dots in the circle, which represent the many things that confront all of us on a regular basis, are still present in this individual's life. But now there is some semblance of order. Stress is still there, but the individual is not "stressed out." Problems are there, but they are handled without caving in to pressure. The "rat race" of moving children from soccer practice to football practice, to play rehearsal, to choir rehearsal, fixing a meal, and getting the car repaired all in the same day—are still very much a part of the daily routine.

But the overwhelming, stress-building, time-consuming, and often aggravating minutia of life are handled in such a way that there is still time to volunteer for ministry, bake a cake for a friend, faithfully attend worship services and Bible study, and yet have an exciting, enriched, and passionate

> *In a working, happy marriage, self has been removed.*

relationship with a spouse. The job, money, education, and everything else is still there, but now there is order in dealing with them because Christ is at the center of their lives. "Self" is out of the picture. **In a working, happy marriage, self has been removed.**

Why is there order? It is because . . . the right relationship is everything! Christ is now on the throne of the individual's life. Self has been removed from the circle, and order and harmony are now predominant. With Christ on the throne, the person now seeks relationships that are wholesome, holy, and productive. Now the individual also has the proper attitude toward his/her sexuality and strives to practice moral purity in the single life.

Let's ask this individual the same series of questions that we asked the residents of circles one and two:

Q.   Who controls your money?

Q. Who controls your time?

Q. Who determines the relationships you maintain with your family and friends?

Q. Where do you attend school?

Q. What about your sexuality?

The answer to every question will be the same: "Christ controls my life."

Living in this circle does not mean that one has reached sinless perfection, or that the mistakes of one's past have all been resolved. Rather, it suggests that one has conquered the major areas of sin in their life. Consequently, whenever one is confronted with a truth that previously has not been embraced, that individual is willing to bring his or her life up to the standard of that biblical truth, while simultaneously raising the standard of their own life.

May I ask you a few rather challenging and confrontational questions? What circle do you live in? Who is on the throne of your life? How is your relationship with God? In order for you to receive the optimal benefit from this book, you must strive for the third circle or, at least, be moving in that direction.

If you are in the first circle, these principles will more than likely seem a bit drastic and even a little ridiculous. Or, if you are a resident of Circle Two, they will be a bit more than you are willing to accept right now as your standard of life. Even if you are living in Circle Three, you very well may find these principles rather narrow and rigid. I am confident, however, that you will do what you always do when faced with challenging biblical truths. You will adjust your life to those standards and be better for it.

After evaluating your relationship with God, you are now ready to be introduced to the **Successful Spouse Selection Process**. This process will take you on a journey that will include four basic steps. This doctrine will show that the unmarried person with the greatest potential for becoming a successful spouse must master four "states" of existence. These are 1) being "Successfully Single." 2) being "Successfully Serving," 3) having "Successful Support Systems," and 4) being "Successfully Submitted." The results of this process produce a marriage rewarded with "Successful Sailing," rather than the bumpy rides encountered by so many others.

The Building Process

A successful marriage, one that stands the test of time, one that spans decades (and not just months or years), the kind that produces a legacy of equally fulfilling and successful relationships, is not built on the shifting sands of "chance." "Chance" says, "We're in love, and that will get us through any and everything we will ever face." But there is often an unstated caveat, "If it doesn't work out, we can always get a divorce." A marriage not initiated on the proper foundational principles, those which are tried, tested, and proven to be timelessly relevant, is a marriage that is playing a game of "chance" with its future survival. As we all know, the foundation of any building rests solely on the proper and adequate construction of the foundation.

The following story serves as a good metaphor for the founding principles of marriage:

Like many other residents of Washington, D.C, during the late 1990s, I watched, with wide-eyed curiosity, the construction of the Ronald Reagan Building. As with all buildings, this one started as a "big hole in the ground." This hole, which was the result of demolition and excavation, was approximately the size of a football field.

As I watched the excavation and foundation work, I wondered: "What was in progress? "What was coming?" For three years it seemed that nothing else was happening except more and more excavation and construction of the foundation. Meanwhile, I changed jobs and did not travel that route for over a year. Finally, one Friday afternoon my commute took me by that particular intersection. To my utter surprise, there stood a building that encompassed a city block. It was an absolute marvel, an example of architectural splendor. I was amazed that the Ronald Reagan Building had been erected in only about a year's time. For a moment, I was surprised by the results of what I remembered—for three years it had been just a "hole in the ground." Now, there stood a building of mammoth proportions.

When thinking about the process of erecting this building, I learned several important principles that can be aptly applied to building a marriage. In constructing the Reagan Building, much of the work was done in the ground. Obviously, this work can be dubbed "groundwork." Likewise, in the process of building a relationship like a marriage, sufficient groundwork must be done even before the foundation can be laid. This groundwork is aptly called "excavation." In the case of the Reagan Building, a previously existing building had to be cleared from the site in order for the work to be completed. Often included in the excavation process is the clearing of "weeds" and "brush."

Many human relationships are similar, in that a previous relationship must first be demolished before the new structure can be built. In most cases, this process is not too difficult, because the old structure was not built on a sturdy or firm foundation. To build good relationships we must first tear down the

> *To build good relationships we must first tear down the old structure before we can proceed with excavation—the groundbreaking work.*

old structure before we can proceed with excavation—the groundbreaking work. In many relationships, however, there are emotional weeds growing everywhere. These "weeds" are the result of bad relationships in the past—hurts, wounds, and scars from ugly breakups. Disappointments and distrust are no longer the size of weeds but are now young saplings.

As a result of being hurt so many times, emotions have become prickly bushes, growing wild across the emotional landscape. In effect, the weeds and unwanted brush symbolize "the fear of loving again." Some of the weeds have been around so long that their roots are running far and wide. They can't be easily removed. Rather, it will take a hoe to pull up their roots. These kinds of feelings must be uprooted to make room for the new landscape to follow: "loving deeply and trusting fully."

This book is designed to begin the process of preparing the "building lot," the persons whose lives the eternal structure of marriage will be built upon. Normally, what begins correctly ends correctly. Let's start off on the right foot and begin our **Successful Spouse Selection** process with some "soil excavation."

CHAPTER 2

Successfully Single

The **Successfully Single Person** is a rare individual in today's world. Such a person has mastered, with great success and finesse, the godly and God-filled single life. Such successful people don't last long in their state of Successful Singleness because they are excellent candidates for marriage. They are the secret envy of everyone—the not so successfully single and even married couples. They have it all—a thriving ministry, a stable job, and extra money in their bank accounts. They have a place to eat at all holidays. They never have to cook, unless they want to. They love children and they find great joy in babysitting a young cousin, sister, or friend's child for an hour, evening, or weekend. They know that such joys are fleeting, and thus they appreciate these moments that much more.

They are well rested. This is because they are able to go to sleep early and wake at the crack of dawn . . . if they want to. They are world travelers, two-seater sports-car drivers, who are always available if a friend needs a shoulder to cry on. This person has a certain aura—a presence.

The almost fairy-tale life of the Successfully Single Person is captured in Genesis 24. In this chapter, we find a model of success that is quite different from how our contemporary society defines success. Its roots are based on strong value systems, character assessment, and principles of morality and family, rather than principles of materialism, financial gain, and personal pleasure.

Genesis 24 begins by revealing to us (after close observation), that Isaac and Rebekah are both living Successfully Single lives in their own respective families, miles apart from each other. Neither of them is actively seeking a mate. They are both living at home, where they have mastered their primary relationships with their parents, siblings, and other family members. Success with these relationships prepares the young couple for enjoying success with subsequent relationships outside of the family. The family is the proving and training ground for learning the proper and appropriate way to handle interpersonal relationships later in life. In other words, Rebekah and Isaac were good children before they became good spouses.

Finding the Right Match

Rebekah is beautiful, yet she is still a virgin, which means that she has been successful in maintaining proper relationships with those of the opposite sex. By all appearances, Rebekah is quite fulfilled in her current state of singleness. With respect to Isaac, Genesis 24 reveals that Abraham, Isaac's father, was more interested in finding Isaac a wife than Isaac was himself. It is Abraham who initiates the process, not Isaac. It is safe to assume then that Isaac was fulfilled in his singleness or, at least, content with waiting on the traditional process for selecting a wife. This process, in which the parents serve as the match-makers, would seem like an antiquated ritual to today's average American.

But let's talk about you and your intended spouse. Where are your afternoons spent? What occupies your lonely hours? Too often, afternoons are spent at "happy hours." Successful Spousal candidates spend more time with their families than in whining (or wining and dining). For the successful single person, the family (biological and spiritual) is the center of his or her social life.

Let me tell you a story of a boy who met a modern-day Rebekah. I must warn you that the male in the story does not at all resemble Isaac. As of the writing of this book, my wife, Mable, and I have been married 35 years. I am tempted to say, "thirty-five glorious years," but that would not be the complete truth. In this regard, Mable certainly has not been the problem, but rather the problem has resided with the author of this book. When I first met Mable, she had recently graduated from high school and had begun a vocational career in the federal government. She had her own "wheels," money, and was genuinely enjoying life without a male suitor. She was taking college classes in the evening, as well as a sewing class. She was not living on her own, but rather shared the house with her mother and two sisters (and was very content in doing so). Of course, I did not know any of this when I met Mable that wonderful Friday evening at the Evangelistic Center in Washington, D.C. I was the musician for a singing group that had been invited to sing at the church's youth revival. After service we (the young people who attended the service) all converged at the center isle and began our introductions. I vaguely remember meeting Mable that evening, but that introduction set the stage for a more formal meeting that was to take place that following Monday afternoon. I was standing on the corner of 13th & "C" Streets waiting for my ride home when Mable walked up to meet others in her car pool. "Didn't we just meet Friday night?' one of us asked, and things began from there.

I will never forget the "phone call," the one when I boldly proclaimed that we should "go out for a bite to eat." I was shocked when Mable did not jump at the idea of going out with this suave, handsome guy who had no car of his own, had not finished high school, and whose job barely paid minimum wage! Of course, she knew none of this. I had not told her these minor details because I was only going out on a date. It never occurred to me that because she was going to have to pick me up, she might suspect that this guy really does not have very much on the ball.

I know what you are probably thinking, "Why would it be an issue who picks up whom?" But remember, this was 35 years ago. I was not concerned in the least that she would be picking me up. All the other young ladies I dated had been more than happy to do so. Instead of giving you all of the details, suffice it to say that Mable was, for all practical purposes, the first Successfully Single young lady I had ever met. She was thoroughly enjoying life before I came along. And, at that stage in my life, as unsuccessfully single as I was, I knew a successfully single woman when I saw one. (I failed to mention that when I tasted her cooking—the deal was sealed!)

Get the picture? Here was a beautiful woman, pursuing a college degree while working a full-time job, who was still living at home helping to support her family. She was not going to single bars frantically looking for a date. She owned her own automobile and was a superb cook. The best part is that I had met her in church, on a Friday night. She had a great relationship with God and was an active member of her church who attended Bible Study and Sunday School. My goodness, what else could a man possibly want or ask for in a woman in 1965? Mable became the most wonderful wife a husband could possibly ask for . . . and it began with her being a Successfully Single Woman.

Now Mable has her own version of our first meeting, which is recounted below.

> *Back then, Pastor Rogers was an interesting mix of character, personality, and let's say "potential." Although he was rough around the edges (which he has so willingly acknowledged), he did have one thing going for him that stood out and really got my attention. He was excited and passionate about his music ministry in his church. Not only did he play the piano for his local church, he was also the pianist for a singing group outside of church. I was also impressed that the Pastor lived at home, helping to support his family. That was commendable. And he had a stable job. Importantly, he had close friends that loved the Lord and were committed to Him. Our first meal together was quite refreshing. Unlike other male suitors, he was able to eat his meal and hold a conversation at the same time. He was not as shy as others whose nervousness prohibited them from eating but a few bites of their meal. In fact, I was quite impressed that the Pastor ate his meal and some of mine! But what really impressed me, and what made me overlook whatever shortcomings he may have had, was what I learned about his family at the holiday meals. It was at those gatherings that the true background and depth of his character was revealed. Not only was the Pastor a very committed Christian, but so were the persons in his immediate and extended family. There were pastors, missionaries, and deacons among the ranks of those gathering at the family meals. This suggested to me that the family had roots of faith in God which ran deep in the life-blood of this young man. Based on what I knew then, he stacked up fairly well.*

At this point, I should elaborate on my definition of the word "success." I use that word in a non-conventional sense, not speaking of material possessions or worldly accomplishments. Instead, I'm referring to the principle that the person you marry needs to be an individual whose life is *emotionally, vocationally,* and *recreationally fulfilled.* His or her time is spent in productive, beneficial activities. He or she has demonstrated the ability to be successful in his or her singleness.

There are five quality traits of the successfully single person. If you are married, these traits also apply to you. In fact, if you have children, start teaching them these traits while they are young.

Characteristics of the Successfully Single Person

*   Character and Integrity

This person has an abundance of character and integrity. Character is what you are when no one is watching or when you don't know someone is watching. Character says, "I do the right thing; you can count on me." Someone has suggested that a commitment is only of value if it comes from a person of character and integrity. Unfortunately, too often we look for the person who, in terms of physical features, is a "10." This human being has it all together on the outside, but inward beauty is much more important (and lasting). A little makeup, a new hairstyle, a workout at the gym, and an updated wardrobe can help the exterior of almost anyone.

Integrity (we can also call this honesty) is the basis of all genuine relationships. What does that person's word mean to him or her? Is that person true to relationships? It is a dreadful experience to be

> *Integrity (we can also call this honesty) is the basis of all genuine relationships.*

married to a person you cannot trust. A very simple test to determine whether an individual is trustworthy is to observe how they handle the following: a person promises to call a friend at a certain time. The call is either not made at the promised time or it is never made at all (you might also observe that the individual makes a habit of not returning calls). The only conclusion is that the individual is not trustworthy and not a man or woman of their word.

*   Humility

Is the individual willing to hear and receive the truth, and can they admit when they're wrong? Does your potential spouse have a teachable spirit? It is so annoying to be around people who are "know it alls." No matter what the subject, this person knows just as much, if not more, than you and everyone else. Does this individual receive instruction that will improve his or her life? One of the key signs of a person of humility is that he or she is willing to admit faults. The best relationships are those in which two people are relentlessly pursuing the truth, especially pertaining to their own strengths and short-comings.

* Intimacy

Does the individual maintain the appropriate amount of emotional involvement for the level of the relationship? Does the person push to get too close too soon? Here is a warning for anyone just beginning a relationship that they hope will last a lifetime: slow your train down or bring it to a screeching halt! Sexual intimacy and the activities that lead to it must be reserved for those who are married. Using this as a standard for moral purity before marriage safeguards your heart and emotions from undue stress and pain often caused by premature emotional and sexual involvement. How many times have you been hurt as a result of a relationship that didn't work out? How many times was your heart torn apart when you tried to sever such relationships? Do not get too close too soon!

* Wholeness

The successfully single person does not consider him or herself needy or unfulfilled but rather a whole person who is well rounded and complete. For this reason, I object to the term "my better half." Instead, I prefer to say "my better whole." This is not to say that someday someone might come into your life that will add to and enhance your existence. But until that happens, your life will be no less fulfilled if you are a whole person.

When I met my wife Mable, she was not a "half person" but was indeed emotionally and psychologically complete and fulfilled. If I called her on the phone it was fine; if I did not call, it was fine. She was pursuing her life's goals and dreams, which she knew she could obtain whether or not a man ever came along. She had developed relationships with other women. She had not put her life on hold waiting for Mr. Right to complete her. Colloquially speaking, Mable "had it all together."

As you are observing someone you are attracted to, you need to take stock of the whole of that person's life: their being, their walk with Christ, and their overall disposition (which should not exude "emptiness"). This single individual should be demonstrating a high degree of stability in his or her life.

*   **Peace**

You want to marry someone who is at peace with his or herself—and the world. Helen Keller, who was deaf and blind, once said, "So much has been given me that I have no time to ponder that which has been denied." After reading this book, if you are single, you should have a different attitude. You will be able to wholeheartedly acknowledge that the Creator has given you so much that you don't have time to think about what you are lacking. Learn to be content—to promote and pursue peaceful surroundings, thoughts, and people.

By the way, someone once said that marriage is a lot like flies at a window: there are some flies trying to get in and some flies trying to get out! A young lady once told me that she had been so satisfied in being single that she never noticed when a young man had been looking at her for some time. It took one of her friends to tell her the guy was "checking her out."

*   **Stability (Sit up for this one!)**

Consistency is the word that comes to mind when I discuss stability. It is not difficult for a person to exercise *sporadic* stability. But what you need to find out is if this person is really stable or flighty . . . here today, gone tomorrow? There is an old hymn that says, "Sometimes I'm up, sometimes I'm down . . . ." If this describes the person you are considering, pause, pause, and pause! Can you depend on and rely on what they say they're planning to do? Sit up! Or are you never quite certain of their daily performance? When they are making a promise to you do you perceive it to be a reliable pledge, or is it just empty words that happened to come from their mouth? Do not overlook this trait, even though appears to be insignificant. Unreliable individuals do unreliable things. Do not ignore this!

Here are a few areas of stability to look for in a potential spouse:

Job Stability

Is this individual able to maintain a steady job? Are they consistently having problems with their supervisors? Do they frequently miss work or are they always on time? Watch out for someone who is bouncing from one job to another and never on a job for more than a year. This could be a sign of a restless person or someone who gets bored easily. This kind of individual often brings this same sense of restlessness into a marriage. They will typically become bored with their spouse and the day-to-day routine of marital life. Too often this leads to the desire to seek excitement and fulfillment outside of the marriage covenant.

Financial Stability

The person who will be your spouse needs to demonstrate a high degree of financial stability. Does he or she live from paycheck to paycheck? How often is the phone turned off? Is a credit card used to pay for even the smallest items? How much money is being saved on a regular basis? Do they have a budget? Most importantly, do they tithe (give a tenth of their income to their local church)?

Before you get too far along with wedding plans, I strongly recommend that you openly discuss yours and your partner's financial history. This should be done before the engagement plans are set. Certainly, there are things that should be kept private in the beginning, such as your social security number and other information that can be used fraudulently (I actually know of this happening). But there must be a time when full financial disclosure is made. If the person baulks, I suggest you put on the brakes! We are aware of several cases in which a spouse was shocked after some months into the marriage to find out that their partner had thousands of dollars in unsecured debt. In one case, it was over $40,000! In the case of children outside of the marriage, when probate courts calculate child support payments, they often increase the amount to reflect the income of the household, not just the single parent.

Assess that person's tangible assets and success at acquiring and maintaining the necessities of life. In this regard, it is prudent to exhibit wise management of one's financial affairs. The wise spender recognizes that a certain percentage of expenditures should be for items that appreciate rather than depreciate.

Try to find out if the person has more financial assets than financial liabilities. Ask this question of yourself: If I marry this person, will he or she arrive with bills or assets? In other words, will you be encumbered with debt that you were not an active participant in creating? As much as is possible, all debt, particularly consumer debt, should be paid off before marriage.

Stability in Relationships Stand up for this one!

Has your potential spouse been successful in maintaining other relationships? Observe whether or not the individual has maintained a relationship with a friend for more than five years. The lack thereof might be an indication that the person has problems forming meaningful relationships. If the best man or maid of honor is someone the individual just met last month, I would run, or at least postpone the marriage until you are more comfortable with this aspect of his or her personality.

Does your potential spouse truly understand the importance, scope, and magnitude of a commitment like marriage? Do you know what the person's attitude toward the marriage commitment will be? What level of commitment does he or she exhibit in relationships with friends and family? If their concept of commitment is misconstrued, marriage may be a significant challenge for them. Because we are creatures of habit, we normally repeat what has become our pattern of life. This includes forming relationships.

The following scenario might be all too familiar to you: you meet a wonderful person that you want to see on a regular basis. You start calling each other with regularity and begin going out to eat and to the movies together. It soon seems that you can't get enough of each other's company. But then one of you does something that drastically changes the relationship.

What happens next serves as a good indication of the potential for success of the relationship. Does the individual "walk" or do they seek to reconcile the fracture in the relationship. However the individual responded to problems in previous relationships is how they will respond when there is a fracture in their marriage. If he or she is accustomed to throwing away a friendship when it turns sour, that will be his or her inclination when they are married. This may not happen the first time trouble sets in. But eventually, the "big one," that big blow up, will occur and that will be the time the individual reverts to past behavior—he or she will leave. That is not the way lasting relationships are maintained.

Another area to observe is the individual's commitment to family. The family is the interpersonal unit that closest resembles a marriage, because you cannot rid yourself of the other individuals in a family. You will be your mother's son or

> *The family is the interpersonal unit that closest resembles a marriage, because you cannot rid yourself of the other individuals in a family.*

daughter and your brother or sister's sibling for the rest of your life. It is in the family setting that you first learn the art of negotiated settlements, better known as resolving conflict.

If your potential spouse does not have a healthy, growing relationship with his or her family, it is probable that he or she won't have a happy marriage. Remember that this person's family has lived with him or her longer than anyone else and has seen the worst and best of that individual, particularly under unguarded conditions. Certainly you understand that dating and even "godly courting" is done under very guarded conditions in a "climate-controlled" environment. Because both people normally allow only their best (or at least their better) sides show, talking to the individual's family candidly and forthrightly is a necessity. A red flag should go up if your potential partner is not on speaking terms with his or her parents.

My wife says that young women need to observe the frequency with which a man is in contact with his family. How often do you hear him say," I'm going to see my parents today." Or, "I'm getting together with my brother tomorrow." Or, "I loaned my sister my car while hers is in the shop for repairs." Are there times when his family's wishes take precedent over your activities together? It is a good thing if he says to you, "I can't do that today, I made a promise to my father/mother/sister/brother/nephew/niece that I would _____."(Fill in the blank as you see fit.) Bear in mind that it is only after marriage that he is biblically obligated to "leave his father and mother and cleave to his wife." As a potential spouse, it is a favorable sign that he sometimes places his family's needs above those you may have as a couple. His family's requests for his time should not result in the *exclusion* of your time together; instead, it should be *inclusive* of your time together. *He* and *they* should begin to view you as a part of the family. From a practical standpoint, the successfully single person needs to have something to offer other than a pretty face or body (such as a strong commitment to Christ, a flourishing ministry, Godly habits, healthy relationships, and/or good credit). Unfortunately, in our western civilization there is an overemphasis on physical beauty. It is an interesting observation that marriages last longer in countries where less emphasis is put on the physical attributes. We are much too "wise" to conclude that there might be some correlation between downplaying the physical and "up" playing the inward. Dare we take it a step further and say that in most Muslim countries, where women reveal none of their physical features, divorce is all but unheard of?

The travesty of selecting a spouse based solely on physical beauty lies in the simple, yet profound notion that everything in life will change over time. We are all in the process of evolving. The negative side of this observation is that a youthful physique will very quickly give way

> *Time improves the admirable and exposes the unfavorable.*

to "middle-age spread" and "old age droop." But from a positive perspective, character, poise, graciousness, manners, respect, and honesty continue to be enhanced with the onset of time and aging. Time improves the admirable and exposes the unfavorable.

Remember, anyone can *get* married, but the goal is *staying* married. That is my desire for you—a happy, fulfilled union that grows in love and romance. A successful marriage is one in which you are still courting each other and where the "thrill" continues. Examine the aforementioned areas of stability very closely when you are considering a lifetime mate.

CHAPTER 3

Successfully Serving

In the last chapter, we learned that in your quest to find a successful spouse, you must observe the degree to which he or she is successfully single. Our focus was on the other person. Now let's turn our attention from the one being observed to the one who is observing. I'm speaking of the person who is reading this book—yes, YOU! This chapter answers the question: how do I know when *I* am ready for marriage? Although the world provides various benchmarks and indicators, you are ready for marriage only when you have mastered the capacity to serve—and to do so joyfully. Thus, this chapter is about developing *the heart of a servant.*

Real and authentic courtship is not about looking for someone who has the right qualities for "spouseship". It is about becoming the right person yourself. Of course, each of us generally considers ourselves to be "a great catch." This is especially true if we're walking closely with the Lord, involved in ministry, have strong family and other relationships, and have a good job. But if we delve into some of the secret corners of our very private and guarded existence, we just might find the truth, good or bad. Who knows "what lurks in the hearts of men and women?" I dare you! Ask your best friend, a family member, preferably a sibling, and a co-worker to write down for you five areas of your life which you need to work on immediately and five areas which you need to work on in the future. Isn't it amazing that our perceptions of who we are vary drastically from the perceptions others have of us?

The challenge before us is how to undo the misguided, self-centered philosophy of the ego-driven society in which we live. This philosophy teaches to all who are seeking marriage that this wonderful, blissful union is for and about YOU. It asks, "What have you done for me lately?" You're certainly not alone if your thinking is similarly misguided. It is interesting that parents who have experienced successful marriages (lasting for more than 20 years) often tell their children that they need to get married to be happy. Actually, they are speaking within the framework of their successful marriage, so they have put the cart before the horse. They have experienced a loving, fulfilling relationship for so long that happiness and marriage become so intertwined that it appears that marriage has been the source of their happiness. But getting married does not, in and of itself, make one happy. There are too many marriages that ended because the husband and wife were not happy. Too often parents are not able to clearly articulate what makes for a successful marriage. They have been happily married for so long that their relationship has become second nature. It is sort of like giving driving directions to your most frequented destination. Recently, Mable was asked directions to get from a friend's church to our church. We were both amused that even though we could travel the route with our eyes closed, we did not know the names of many of the streets. We ended up looking on the Internet to get directions. It is the same with many successful marriages—they are successful, but the success is often unexplainable.

Are you laboring under the false notion that you get married so that YOU can be happy? If you are, pray and ask God to help you change your thinking. If you don't change, you are destined to fail. There are three proper reasons to get married, which I discuss below.

Reason 1:

*   **To dedicate your life to making your *mate* happy.**

This means you find happiness and joy when you see them happy and fulfilled. Your greatest joy in life is knowing that you have done something that pleases your spouse and that makes him or her more comfortable and contented. This is the proper attitude one should have toward the marriage relationship. Love's direction is always outward. When love is turned inward, we have the potential for selfishness, greed, and self-centeredness.

Our heavenly Father's love for us was demonstrated in giving us His son to die for the sins of the world (John 3:16). Sadly, too often we have confused love with lust. Love asks, "What can I do for you?" But lust asks, "What can and will you do for me?" Love asks, "What can I give you?" Lusts asks, "What can and will you give me?"

Once inward love has been redirected to outward love, the next step is to marry someone who has the same commitment to

> *Once inward love has been redirected to outward love, the next step is to marry someone who has the same commitment to loving in the proper manner that you have.*

loving in the proper manner that you have. That individual must also acknowledge that he or she is willing to make a lifelong commitment toward making you happy.

Reason 2:

*   **To mutually complement one another.**

God said in Genesis 2:18, "It's not good that the man should be alone, I will make a helper suitable for him"—or compatible with him (or, even better, a complement to him). When I get dressed, I usually prefer to wear clothes with contrasting colors. I like a red or burgundy tie with a blue or gray suit; I rarely wear a blue necktie with a blue suit. I like the difference the contrasting colors add to the outfit. Similarly, God created the woman to complement the man, giving him someone whose personality contrasts with his own. An introverted person will inevitably be paired with an extrovert. The introvert is generally the individual who enjoys their private space and solitude. If they have their druthers, most of their time would be shared one-on-one with their mate. On the other hand, the extroverted mate is happy when a crowd is around. They are bored with solitude.

It is God's intention, by pairing these dissimilar individuals, that there would be a wonderful balance between the two of them. But another interesting twist to the contrasting personality theory is that God created the woman enough like the man to allow harmony within their contrasting natures. For the most part, the husband approaches life in terms of a goal or task, whereas the wife typically views life through the relationships she creates. When the wife disagrees with the husband on some given subject, the wise man knows that for the husband to make a well balanced decision, he must understand the perspective his wife brings to the subject. He needs this understanding no matter how unnerving, farfetched, and disconcerting her perspective appears at the moment.

In a successful marriage, the husband and wife view their differences as assets rather than liabilities. Successful couples have learned to appreciate their differences, not just tolerate them. These differences bring balance to the relationship. One of the joys of marriage is to find out that not only did you marry a handsome or beautiful mate but someone who has the strengths to compensate for your specific weakness.

When we combine the first and second reasons for marriage, our commitment to our spouse can be described as follows: I have found someone to whom I want to give the rest of my life bringing happiness, and I am willing to do whatever it takes to make him

> *I have found someone to whom I want to give the rest of my life bringing happiness, and I am willing to do whatever it takes to make him or her happy and fulfilled in life.*

or her happy and fulfilled in life. I realize I have the capability of helping this individual. I can best help and serve my intended spouse by complementing his or her deficiencies, because I have strengths that compensate for my partner's weaknesses.

It is astounding to see how far we have deviated from this commitment today. God created the husband and wife to complement each other, not to compete with each other. God never intended for the man and the woman to compete for the same job. It is clear in the way that God designed, shaped, and built the man and the woman. The designer had different tasks in mind. The man and the woman's body, mind, and emotions, lend themselves to having contrasting skills, producing differing "resumes." Each gender has a different constitution, idiosyncrasies, and distinctions that lend themselves to an endless array of complementing opportunities. Therefore, the second purpose for marriage is to mutually complete one another.

Reason 3:

*   **To multiply a godly legacy.**

After God blessed the man and the woman, the next thing He said to them was "have some children"—and have a lot of them. Make plans to have or adopt children. This is the third reason for marriage. Contrary to contemporary western culture, the most important thing a couple can do in life is not to live in a half-million dollar house, drive an expensive European automobile, or amass great wealth. Rather, the most important thing you can do in life is to raise a child or children who will positively impact the world in which they live. The joy of being a parent is knowing that, long after you are gone from this world, your legacy will live on. This legacy is more important than the many accoutrements (i.e. economic status, a house, a car, a job) of life in which our society places great value. Here's a worthwhile principle to remember when you get married: *God is always working on the next generation.*

As you contemplate the three proper reasons for marriage, do you notice that YOU are conspicuously missing? You and your desires and wishes have been intentionally left out. It is a legitimate right and expectation for you to have needs, to want to satisfy your desires and aspirations; however, you must understand that they are not to be your focus or concern but the focus and concern of your wife. Marriage must be the most unselfish act of love you have ever experienced. The first major adjustment many young married adults must conquer in marriage is *selfishness.* It usually first shows its ugly head when our spouse fails to make us happy. Here is a little secret about happiness: you can always be happy if your happiness is derived from the joy you bring to your spouse. Suddenly, your happiness is under *your* control. If happiness is left to the whim of a spouse, however, you might end up waiting and wanting until they are in the mood to make you happy. Take full advantage of this prescription for "anytime happiness." Take regular large doses of it. You cannot overdose on this. In fact, intoxication from this prescription is recommended.

What Serving Looks Like

Successfully serving (by seeking for the good of the other) means that you must be willing to give up your plans and dreams so your partner can be happy.

As I am writing this segment of my book, I am waiting for Mable to pick me up from my church office. It is a Saturday—a rare Saturday because I am not preaching at The Triumphant Church on Sunday. These Saturdays are a scarcity for me. If this were football, it would be called a "bye week"—

a week off. Understand that as a pastor of a church, the primary focus for me every week is next Sunday's sermon. Normally, Saturdays are days in which my mind is preoccupied with the delivery of the sermon. So when I do not have to preach on a Sunday, I can relax and enjoy my Saturday.

This particular Saturday, Mable and I planned to have a day where we could do whatever we wanted. You see, the last three consecutive Saturdays we had been conducting marriage or singles' workshops. So we were looking forward to our Saturday off together. Everything was right on schedule until late Friday night. Pat, a dear friend of the family, called Mable. She had an appointment Saturday at 11 a.m. in Alexandria, Virginia (which is about 45 minutes from our house). In order for Pat to get to that appointment on time, she would have to leave extremely early and ride three buses to her destination. Mable asked if I would allow her to take Pat to her appointment, which would alter our morning plans. I said that would be all right, since we would still have most of the day left to ourselves.

When I realized that Mable was not going to be driving by herself, I thought about how dirty the car was. I certainly could not let her pick up her friend in a junky car. So while she was getting ready, I washed the car as quickly as I could (I literally wiped down the rubber bumpers and wheels as she drove out of the driveway). There was still plenty of the day left. The one exception to my carefree day was to rehearse with the Men's Chorus at 1 p.m. With that in mind, we decided that I could ride to church with a member of the choir who lives near us. That way, we would be able to continue our day of freedom in one car.

As I was getting dressed, I began thinking how much nicer it would be for Mable if she, Pat, and Linda (another friend who was visiting from Cleveland, Ohio), could go out to eat after Pat's appointment. I had intended to call her and let her know that I could stick around the church for awhile but had not gotten around to it. When I got to church, she had already returned from taking Pat to her appointment. Mable said that Pat and Linda really wanted her to go out to eat with them at our favorite restaurant, *The Cheesecake Factory*.

Mable decided not to go because she knew I had planned for us to be together this Saturday (reverse psychology, perhaps?). Did I mention that we had even coordinated our attire for the day? She had no idea that I anticipated that the three of them would want to have lunch together. I stated, "Honey, you go while I rehearse with the men and I will wait here until you get back. I can work on the book until you pick me up."

In my mind, I thought I would be picked up by 2 p.m. or at the latest, 3 p.m. It is now 6 p.m. as I write this and I continue to wait. You must believe me—I am sincerely happier (that she is enjoying herself) by waiting on my wife's return, knowing that she and her girlfriends are laughing and acting crazy, while I am waiting in my office—planned day gone. In fact, I am so elated that they are having a ball that I can't wait to hear all about it. That will be all the joy I need for today!

If this should happen to someone who has not mastered the art of successfully serving, right about now—at 6 p.m.—there is steam coming out of their ears. There will be words expressed that go something like this, "How could you do this to me? You know I had planned this day." This is a tricky accusation because what they are actually accusing the

> *The heart of a servant thinks and seeks for the good of the one who is the object of his or her affection.*

other person of is, in reality, what they have been guilty of themselves. "How could you be so selfish to think only of yourself when you knew what I wanted to do?" **The heart of a servant thinks and seeks for the good of the one who is the object of his or her affection.**

Have you noticed it yet? Marriage is really an "others-centered" relationship. Before you become overly discouraged by this rather shocking approach to marriage (which may seem to completely exclude you from any direct benefit from the marital union), be reminded that you are on the other side of the table from the person you are courting. It is the responsibility of your intended spouse to seek your ultimate happiness and well being. Certainly, one goal in getting married is for you to be happy and fulfilled. And it is likewise a priority to have your emotional, physical, and social needs met. But it is my desire that they not be met, sought, or initiated by you, but rather by your mate.

How is the heart of a servant exemplified in the day-to-day routine of a single person? They are involved in serving others on a regular basis. The person seeking marriage should learn this wonderful, but lost art. If this is not your forte, it is not entirely your fault. You happen to have been raised in a materialistic and self-centered society. You have been incorrectly taught to look out for number one.

A joyous, fruitful life is a life that is directed toward serving others. Jesus Christ helps us understand this when He tells us He did not come to be served but to serve (Matthew 20:28). You have not lived until you have given your life away! There are many, many, ways to serve, but the focus has got

> *You have not lived until you have given your life away!*

to be off of you. Think of ways to do for others in every facet of your life (i.e., how can I serve others in my ministry, with my time, with my resources, at my job, with my hobbies, with my gifts . . . ?). As a single person, you can easily become selfish with your time, your car, your plans, and your money. If you get married with that attitude, your marriage will be in trouble!

Once while Mable and I were presiding over a Singles Ministry meeting, a young man asked a familiar question. It is a recurring theme among those seeking marriage. "When do I know that I am ready for marriage?" Mable gave the best answer to this question that I have ever heard. This was her response: Do not even think of getting married until you are ready to "give your life away". You are ready to be married only when you are ready to dedicate your life to pursuing the happiness of your mate. Are you ready for marriage?

Developing the Heart of a Servant

Try to develop the heart of a servant. Just think about this for a moment: What did you do this week for someone other than yourself? As busy as you were last week, how much of that busy-ness was in accomplishing something for someone other than yourself? The shopping cart was full. Was there anything in it for anyone other than you? You washed and waxed your car. Now, what about your sister's car? Ask anyone who is experiencing a happy life with their soul mate, and they will tell you this simple but profound truth: a happy marriage is the result of two people willing to serve each other with joyful hearts.

Parents, teach your little children to say these words more often: "Mom (or Dad), is there anything I can do for you today?" To develop the heart of a servant, try this sometime. Telephone your parents and inform them in your customary manner of your plans for the holiday weekend. But then tell them that before following through on these plans, you just want to see if there is something they need you to do and, if so, you will put off your plans. Try the same thing on a friend or sibling. Ask, "Do you need me to do anything for you today?" In fact, sometimes don't even ask. Just go by and wash the car for them. Call Mom, Dad, or a retired church member and inform them, "I'm coming over to cut your grass for you." I cannot count the times I have had persons ask, "Do you need me to do anything for you?" only to have them walk away before I could answer.

Recently, one of the deacons of The Triumphant Church caught me off guard when he asked, "Pastor, do you need me to do anything?" That was not unusual, but what followed was totally unexpected. He just stood there, waiting for a response. I've grown accustomed to folks asking: "Pastor, if you need me to do anything, call me." It became obvious to the deacon by the look of disbelief on my face that he had caught me off guard and had really put me on the spot. So he said to me, "I'll wait in the church office while you think about it, and I'll come back to check in a few minutes." That is the heart of a servant.

Another example is Johnny, a single young man who works at an elementary school with another dear church member and friend, Francina. I had previously met him but was reacquainted with him on the night Fran's uncle passed away. Fran's uncle had been diagnosed with cancer about a year before his death. Fran had taken on the added responsibility of trying to care for him at his home rather than sending him to a nursing home.

Perhaps it is appropriate to digress for a moment to talk about Francina. In the dictionary beside the words "heart of a servant" appears Fran's picture—single mom, divorcee, and servant of God and mankind. She has dedicated her life to serving others. The interesting result of her devoted service is her uncanny ability to solicit help from normally unwilling participants. It is known among the members of The Triumphant Church that if Fran can get you cornered, she can get you to do anything the church needs done. People run from her (this often includes me), because the word is out that if she asks you, you're hooked—you cannot say no. The reason is that everyone sees her selfless life and knows that what she does is done for the good of others. That disposition is irresistible, intoxicating, and compelling.

But, back to Johnny. I was wondering why he was at Fran's home that night, so I inquired if he was a member of the family. I was told who he was and the role he had played in the last months and days of her uncle's life. He had helped Fran by spending many nights and days with her uncle, often staying all night when he did not want to be left alone. These are but two shining examples of many who have developed what I refer to as the "heart of servant."

Learn to carve out time for others. Acquire the ability to drop what you have planned to do and rearrange your schedule for someone else. I've been married for more than 30 years. Over those years, I've learned to cancel my plans and joyfully accommodate my spouse when she needs me. I may not get to do what I had planned until next week, the week after, or maybe never. But that's what the happy and fulfilled life of an individual with the heart of a servant looks like.

Ways to Practice Service to Others

- ❖ Volunteer to baby-sit (free of charge) for a single parent
- ❖ Wash your mother's car
- ❖ Visit an elderly neighbor or relative and insist on completing a cleaning project or running an errand for them
- ❖ Join a ministry in which you serve others on a regular basis
- ❖ Volunteer in the community
- ❖ Make it a point to ask someone if they need help with anything EVERY day
- ❖ When you go shopping for yourself, change the plan and buy something for someone else instead

CHAPTER 4

Successfully Submitting

If we can, we should imagine the process of choosing a spouse and building a lifelong relationship as being similar to the weaving of individual strands of wool in a hand woven rug. But if we look more closely, we see one color that needs to be added. This particular hue (or shade) is the idea of "successful submission." The word submission has negative connotations in our society today. Most women cannot stomach the thought of a man telling them what to do. Likewise, most men don't understand the importance of willfully submitting to their wives. After all, men have been told repeatedly by other Bible toting husbands that the wife is to submit to her husband. We will unravel this misinterpretation of scripture in just a moment. But for now, let's develop the proper attitude and understanding of the concept of submission. Submission, in its purest form, really has to do with protection. A successful marriage just does not work without submission and accountability.

> *A successful marriage just does not work without submission and accountability.*

Submission is the voluntary process that allows someone to take part in the decisions you make in your life. It is the willfulness to consider the advice of another as necessary and beneficial to the successful completion of your plans, whatever or whoever they may involve. It is this awareness, solicitation, and yielding to the input of another person that allows others to come into your life. The Scriptures help us understand this concept of submission.

> *In the Lord, however, woman is not independent of man, nor is man independent of woman. For as woman came from man, so also man is born of woman. But everything comes from God.*
>
> (I Corinthians 11:11-12)

Mable and I believe that when God created man and woman, he created them with the capacity to view the world from differing points of view. His plan was that there would be a woman in each man's life and a man in each woman's life. God created Adam and then created Eve after observing that Adam's existence was incomplete without Eve. God actually uses a phrase that here-to-fore had not been used: "it is not good . . . ."

> *The Lord God said, "It is not good for the man to be alone. I will make a helper suitable for him."*
>
> (Genesis 2:18)

When an individual comes to realize the benefits of submission, then the "idea" of submission must find some external manifestation. Accountability is the external manifestation of the principle of submission. Submission is a way of thinking, or a state of mind. Accountability, then, is submission in action. Accountability involves choosing an individual with whom you have a relationship, to whom you will submit to in various areas of your life.

Submission in Action

Even though the process of submission applies to both genders, in marriage, obviously, it becomes a very gender-specific matter. This often complicates the issue even more, and it is why couples struggling with the demands of submission and accountability should resolve the issue before getting married. The best place to get accustomed to submission and accountability between men and women is in the family. Hopefully, there will be males and females in the family structure. If not, the individual should seek out gender diversity in

> *The best place to get accustomed to submission and accountability between men and women is in the family.*

the extended family of uncles, aunts, cousins, and so on. If all other family structures fail in providing the proper venue for gender specific submission, God, in His wise providence, has provided the church family structure to serve as the training ground for "submitting ourselves one to another" Ephesians 5:21.

When a husband does not learn how to successfully submit before getting married, he will likely be shocked the first time his darling little wife naively asks, "Honey, where have you been?" or "Where are you going?" I'm sure that many of you are familiar with the answer. "What do you mean, where have I been?" Or, the wife who has been accustomed to spending her money on whatever she wants, whenever she wants, is now queried by her husband when he gets the new monthly credit card bill, "Honey, what did you buy for $200 last Saturday at Macy's?" A spouse who has been successfully submitting will be able to avoid potentially damaging scenes like these.

My wife, Mable, offers two excellent examples of the concept of Successful Submission in action:

> One of the women at our church has chosen to be accountable and submit herself to me for advice and spiritual guidance. A few months ago, she received her income tax refund in the mail. I knew in advance the check would be coming soon, and I had asked her about it. I did not want her to spend the money on unnecessary things, because we both knew that she had sufficient monthly income to get everything she needed. Instead, I had planned to advise her to invest the check in a safe investment, such as a savings bond. After the check arrived and I discussed this with her, she literally pleaded with me to let her keep some of the money. The sight of a 40-year-old woman pleading for something she really didn't need was hard to watch or understand. Eventually, the woman released the check to me. On the surface it would seem that the young woman was not Successfully Submitting. But remember that she did not have to give me the check. She realized that I was acting with her best interest in mind.

> Another example of the benefits of submission is the story of a young man in our church who was struggling to manage his money. As a result, he solicited help from one of our female ministry leaders, Valjean Miller (Valjean heads our unofficial "Get out of Debt" Ministry). To the young man's surprise, and perhaps dismay, Valjean was very demanding of him to get his house in order (even though she has the perception of being a rather mild-mannered individual). But because of his willingness to surrender his financial management to Valjean, he was able to regroup, re-coop, and rebound from his dismal financial situation. His situation improved so much that he even began to pay his rent a month ahead of time!

The person who has conquered submission like our two examples above is the safest person for you to marry. Even if they do not have all their ducks in a row, a willingness to submit to a godly person with their best interests at heart indicates that they will probably fare well in marriage.

The Challenge

It is quite interesting to see the adjustment many new members of The Triumphant Church make when they first join our church family. Many are not prepared to become a part of a community in which they will be challenged in their personal and private lives. Very often people are taken aback when someone lovingly confronts and challenges them concerning certain personal behaviors: "That's not the right thing for you to do . . . that's not the right way for you to live . . . or I want you to pray about working on this area in your life." We live in a society that teaches us to be independent. "I'm my own man . . . Be your own woman. Don't let anybody in your space." It's uncomfortable when somebody comes and gets in your space and tells you, "We're not going to let you live like that because we love you."

In Genesis 24:18, Rebekah understood the principle of submitting even while she was single. Consider how she submitted to her family and observe areas of her life in which she practiced submission. In her case, her submission was particularly necessary because she was contemplating marrying a man whom she had never met. She had only met the servant of the man she was being asked to marry. Even though those of you reading this book may never experience this type of pre-arranged marriage, there is a principle to be gleaned. There is much about the individual you are considering to marry that has yet to be revealed and, in many cases, is actively being concealed. The wise person looks to his or her support system or "covering" (in this case, the family) for a deeper level of character revelation. There are five ways that Rebekah's covering—her family, including her brothers—assisted her (and can also assist you).

*   Visual Evaluation

After learning of the possibility of a marriage between his sister and Isaac, Laban immediately went to evaluate Isaac. (Genesis 24:29-30). In other words,

Laban demonstrated that physical appearances are important—he checked him out visually. Your covering needs to do the same thing: visually check out the person you intend to marry. There are some things that you can observe just by looking at a person. Body language alone reveals a great deal.

I suggest that a woman observe the following about her prospective husband: Is he a gentleman? Does he open the door for ladies? Is he polite, courteous, helpful, never rude or obtrusive? Is he flirtatious? Observe his eyes and head when a rather attractive woman passes within eye sight. Is he actively involved in a ministry in the church? Is he flashy in his appearance and manner of dress? Does he like to show off wads of money? Also, watch out for a lot of earrings and tattoos.

There are also a number of things Mable believes that a man should watch for in a prospective wife. They include the following: Is she boisterous in her manner of speaking? Is her style of dress sexy and provocative or do her clothes accentuate her femininity? Is there a grace and poise in how she walks, sits, and stands? Watch out for tattoos, excessive jewelry, ostentatious hair styles, tight jeans, shirts that show her stomach, short skirts, and women who smack gum in an unlady-like fashion.

We realize, of course, that human beings look on the outward appearance but God looks on the heart. And, yes, the real essence of a person is on the inside; but until we can unearth that part of the person, we've got to go with what we can see.

* Home Evaluation

Laban invited Isaac into their home (verse 31) because the home is a safe environment for a woman (particularly a young woman) to interact with a potentially future husband. It is what we call a "controlled environment."

Dating has evolved out of a "calling" system. This intentionally safe system evolved when the young man came "calling" on the young lady. He came to her house and was invited into the living room to sit on the couch—he on one end and she on the other. The mother and father would most often be in the dining room or another room close by. Isn't it interesting that during this time in history, when relationships were developed under the shadow and close eye of parents and family, there was very little premarital pregnancy? But since the "calling" system was cast aside for the more conventional procedure called dating, premarital pregnancy has become rampant.

According to Dr. Don Raunikar, author of *Choosing God's Best*, there were even fewer emotionally scarred women when the calling system of courting was in place. Dr. Raunikar describes his reasoning as follows:

> *The home was a safe haven for the young lady as well as the young male. Subsequently, modern day society moved to the "dating/rating" system. When groups of individuals began migrating to the city, they started doing something called "going out." The young man would come and take the young lady out. When the young ladies were taken out of the home, they were taken out of a safe, controlled environment.*[1]

The word *home* is not necessarily just the physical place where you live; instead, it represents a group of people who have your best interest at heart. They are those who are mature enough to guard you from the blindness of infatuation or, for that matter, love. It was at this time that young women became very vulnerable, because they did not have the protection they so desperately needed. Maybe some of you need to go back to the safe environment of the home.

* Verbal Evaluation

Rebekah's brother listened closely and evaluated the statements of Eliezer (verses 33-49). He listened to what Eliezer said as he told the story of how Abraham had sent him on this mission. You know what Laban was doing? He was checking out Eliezer's "line." You need to have someone who can objectively evaluate what your potential mate is saying. While they are espousing their good intentions and claiming to be honorable, they may have other motives. As such, you need someone else to validate their claims.

* Spiritual Evaluation

Perhaps the most noteworthy observation by Rebekah's covering was their conclusion that the hand of the Lord was in the matter of her marriage (verse 50). Whoever serves as a covering for you, preferably your parents and your extended family, needs to observe whether or not the hand of the Lord (the presence and the blessing of God) is evident in the relationship that you're contemplating. No matter how you feel, this is the overriding concern that needs to be recognized by the people who make up your support system (i.e., your parents). They are not concerned about the goose bumps on the back of your neck. More importantly, they want to know if God is in the development and substance of the relationship. Is this a "God-blessed thing?" No matter how good it appears to be, if the marriage is not God's perfect will for your life, it is something you should not want, as well.

*   The Pronouncement of Blessing

Marriage should only occur with the blessing of the family. If the family does not approve of the marriage, it should be postponed until such time as the parents will agree to it. Mable and I have counseled many couples who revealed that one of the mothers of the couple had themselves been divorced twice, leaving the parent bitter and resentful toward men. One young person began to share what they were learning with the mother who opposed the relationship and actually ministered to that parent. Having had her issues sufficiently addressed, the mother not only approved of the marriage but paid for the expenses.

Principles of Submission and Accountability

The first thing you must understand about the words accountability and submission is that they relate to protection, not authority and domination. Don't let secular and worldly definitions and associations confuse you. Submission, as opposed to domination, is always voluntary.

In their book, *Moments Together for Couples,* Dennis and Barbara Rainey discuss several characteristics of the "unaccountable." *The unaccountable are people who go through life doing their own thing and as a result of this attitude; their lives are in bad shape.* See Appendix A for the characteristics of the unaccountable.

There are six areas in your life where you might need protection:

(1) You need protection from yourself.

We are our own worst enemy. If we can ever get ourselves straight, then we'll be able to help get somebody else straight. Let me refer you to Romans 7, where Paul said, "When I would do good, evil is always present." There is a war going on inside, thus you need someone who is a "covering" in your life to help you and often protect you from yourself. There are many bad circumstances that you can get into that will make your life a mess if you are not accountable to someone else. Too often, we want to do what we want to do (and when we want to do it). Therefore, we end up being our biggest problem. You need a person to submit to, who will confront you, get in your face and say to you that you're not going to do that any more. Ultimately, you need protection, first of all, from yourself.

(2) You need protection from your heart.

> *Above all else, guard your heart, for it is the wellspring of life.*
>
> (Proverbs 4:23)

> *The heart is deceitful above all things and beyond cure. Who can understand it?*
>
> (Jeremiah 17:9)

It is so easy for your heart to get involved when you are in a close relationship with someone. Your heart gets involved and you really think it's love; but very often it's not love, it's infatuation. The heart is unable to use sound judgment in its assessments. By nature it is superficial and flawed.

The heart always seems to be captured and drawn away by "soulish" and emotional tantrums. The heart is captivated by what is on the surface. It is ill-equipped to perceive the core of an individual, which is character. Have you ever met a person who was involved with someone who has a life controlling habit? They were clearly aware of this condition, yet still "fell in love". Others you have known have fallen in love with individuals who are involved with multiple lovers and yet still plan to marry them. It is the heart that causes them to do these things.

The scriptures warn us that our hearts will "mess us up" if we follow our hearts only. Thus, there is the need to guard against getting too close too soon. Keep the relationship at arms length until ample scrutiny and observation has been applied in all areas—especially the matter of character. Dating, going out together, late night phone calls, and of course, physical intimacy all open the heart up to hurt and pain.

(3) You need protection from ego.

This is perhaps more a male need than a female one. We as men need to be protected in the area of our egos. So many times young men get in trouble because they let their egos rule.

I was recently talking to one of my pastor friends who had gotten into a terrible argument with a teacher in his church. The teacher differed with him on certain interpretations of scripture. Reaching no resolution in the matter, the teacher said he was going to leave the church. My friend became extremely angry (almost violently) over the phone. His wife had to come in and pull him off the phone. It was all about ego. Apparently, the teacher had said some things about the pastor that were not true. I suggested that, in the future, he should call me before he gets into this kind of argument. Then, we could discuss what he intended to say before actually talking to the person. He said, "You know what Tommy, that's what I'll do." In other words, he would submit to me in that area. The truth of the matter is that (as a matter or practice) we both submit to each other. That is why I was able to confront him during this time of crisis. Note that his submitting was for his protection. Do you know how many people, especially males, have gotten into fights and even killed somebody simply because someone "disrespected" them? We need to be protected in the area of our egos.

(4) You need protection from your emotions.

According to Mable, whereas men struggle more in the area of their ego, women are more vulnerable in the area of emotions. Most women, if they will be honest, have made regretful decisions because they were overcome with emotion (i.e., anger, hurt, fear, or love). Too many times, women are hurt in relationships because their emotions are more involved than their male counterparts. More often than not, the male views the woman as an object to be conquered. Normally, it is the woman that hears wedding bells first, because she is the first to get emotionally attached. The rational, logical man puts the woman in the category of his job, his car, his finances, etc. His view of the relationship is a compartmentalized, necessary, and useful part of his existence. Generally speaking, if he loses the relationship, it is the same to him as the loss of a job, house, or car. They cut their losses and move on.

But, for the woman, her heart has grown attached by the words he has said to her, the intimate dinners they have shared, and the affection he has shown. She clings to him because he is meeting her number one emotional need, affection. She will do whatever it takes to continue having that need met, no matter what it cost. She is not realizing that these escapades were merely the adventures of a hunter tracking his prey.

(5) You need to be protected spiritually.

Hebrews 13:17 gives us important biblical insights into spiritual accountability and reveals that you must obey your leaders and submit to their authority. Acts 20:28 tells the apostles to guard the flock of God over which the Holy Spirit has made them overseers. Let me tell you the reason why a pastor is so important to you and why you need to be careful about choosing one. The pastor is looking out for the eternal you. The dentist looks out for your teeth so they won't come out prematurely, the cardiologist looks out for your heart so that you stay healthy as long as possible, and the neurologist takes care of your nervous system. But the pastor has the awesome responsibility of caring for your eternal being.

Another way to look at this is that the waiter brings you food, but you're going to be hungry later; the mechanic fixes your car that's going to break down eventually; but the minister and teacher, however, are the only persons who are taking care of what is going to last you for an eternity. Ministers and Bible teachers are not just giving you food that will be replaced tomorrow with hunger. The food you receive from them is going to determine where you will spend eternity. And the Bible says you need to submit to the leaders of the church or whatever place of worship you are apart of because they are watching out for the "eternal you."

(6) You need to be protected from youthful lusts.

There's a saying that youth is wasted on the young. When I was 18 I thought I knew everything. I thought my mother didn't know a thing, that she was so out of touch. Most of the time, when she would tell me something I would think, "Oh, she doesn't know what she's talking about." But the older I got, the smarter she got! If only I could have known as a young person what I have learned through experience!

Young people need a covering, someone to be accountable to and to protect them from youthful lusts and desires. When I remember the stuff that I thought was so important as a young person, I am simply amazed. For example, I thought it was so important for me to have a big shiny new car, and it had to be clean all the time. I also thought I had to have alligator shoes and custom-made shirts. I thought all that stuff was important. Now the car is filthy; it hasn't been washed in two weeks (but, I still like quality clothing).

Accountability

Every man and woman needs a spiritual covering and there should be many people in your life to answer that need. First and foremost, there is your family. You need to maintain a healthy, ongoing relationship with your family. Even if they are un-churched, they still have wisdom that is beneficial and profitable to you. Listen to your parents, listen to your siblings, listen to your aunts, uncles, and grandparents. For they really know you and are a covering for you. But, there is also your church family and you need to listen to them as well. They are looking out for the eternal you, and they also care and love you. Likewise, there should be mature friends and others in your lives who are genuinely concerned about you— who will look out for your well being and have your best interest at heart.

Secondly, every man needs to have a leader (or coach) within the body of Christ, to whom he submits. There needs to be some godly male leader to whom you are submitted. Men need protection in the area of their egos. Godly and mature men and women are always submitted to godly leadership in the church. Observe the leadership of your local assembly and find a person to whom you should submit yourself.

When you have someone to whom you are accountable and to whom you must answer, it will help alleviate the possibility of you doing whatever you wish. When the people who are

> *When you have someone to whom you are accountable and to whom you must answer, it will help alleviate the possibility of you doing whatever you wish.*

closest to you and to whom you are accountable constantly tell you the same thing (without any of them knowing what the other is saying), that could very well be God speaking to you through their words. If there are several persons to whom you have submitted who agree that the person you want to marry is not the right choice for you, it is safe to assume that God is speaking to you!

The person to whom you are accountable must be "accountable to God for you" (Hebrews 13:17). This individual must be accountable to God when they give you advice. They also need to be praying for you under the fear of God. Be careful when advice is given too quickly. The best response is, "Let me pray about this and get back to you." Those who pause to say this understand that the advice they are giving you will be taken seriously and obeyed. Before they tell you to do something, you must know that they have talked to God, have sought God, and have determined that this is God's will for your life.

Thirdly, because you have made yourself accountable to this person, if you heed their advice and it turns out that their council was wrong, you need to be able to "blame up." If something goes wrong (as a result of their instruction), you want to be able to say, "Well, my covering said . . . the person that I am submitting to said . . . . You need to be able to appeal to God knowing that you sought council from your covering first. Here's a scenario: You have found someone who you are willing to submit to. You have gone to them for advice on a certain matter. They give you advice and you execute the plan of action. But it turns out that the advice is erroneous. Hebrews 13:17 says, ". . . they must give an account." A great example of this biblical principle of accountability (extending to those who exercise leadership) is seen in the responsibility of parents with their children. Parents are responsible for their children's education, social behavior, spiritual, and physical health up to at least age 18. Our society holds the parents responsible for the failing of their children unless there are extenuating circumstances. Likewise, God holds leaders responsible for the misguided actions of the followers.

A rather practical example of this principle occurred while writing this book. My wife and I were flying home from South Africa. We left 45 minutes late because there were technical problems with the aircraft. Over 300 passengers had to be inconvenienced for a decision made by one man, the captain. We submitted to his decision because we understood his position of authority. If anything were to have gone wrong, the captain is ultimately held responsible. Our lives were dependent upon his experience in piloting the aircraft, and fortunately, we all arrived safely.

Lastly, it is extremely important to choose the person to whom you will be accountable when the weather is fair. Do not choose them in the middle of a storm. When a storm arises, you need to have the relationship already in place. Likewise, when the weather is sunny, you will not realize the significance of their role in your life. While the weather is fair, you can objectively see your "accountability person" for who they are.

Look at the third verse of scripture in the last book of Judges. In this book, the Israelites went through a vicious cycle. They would do right for a little while. Then they would go away from God. God would punish them and send the heathen nations to chastise them. Israel would go through the same cycle over and over again. One of the saddest verses of scripture is: "In those days Israel had no king; everyone did as he saw fit." (Judges 21:25)

You see, the problem in America today is that there is so much disorder. Everyone does what is right in their own eyes. Where there is no authority, there is no order. Where there is no order, there is no anointing. The anointing is God's blessing and approval on your life. If you really want to be blessed of God, you've got to get in order and you have to submit to those who are in authority. The anointing always starts from the head and proceeds downward.

Consider the man who was around the pool of Bethesda (John 5). If he had gotten in the water at the right time, when the blessings were coming, he would have been healed long before the time he met Jesus. Are you out of order? Are you doing your own thing? Are you going to church when you feel like going? Giving when you want to give? Paying your tithes when you want to pay them? Praying when you want to pray? Living the way you want to live? Dressing the way you want to dress? Well, you go ahead, but don't think you're going to experience the blessing of God because you are out of order!

The anointing flows from the head; it doesn't start over on the side. He doesn't anoint an arm with oil. He anoints the head. You need to purpose in your heart that you are going to submit to authority. You need to begin asking advice before you start making decisions because you understand that authority and submission have to do with protection and you want to be protected.

CHAPTER 5

Successful Support Systems

This chapter is about what I have dubbed the "topsoil" of marital relationships. The environment in which we typically live is not relationally rich. Often, negative environmental issues threaten the relationships that attempt to exist. There are several things that must be done in a relationship in order to produce rationally healthy individuals, and thus people are able to become successful spouses.

Let me illustrate this point. In the past, Mable and I have been unsuccessful in planting and growing a garden. No blame should be placed on the flower garden. We really just didn't know what we were doing. We invested in plants and flowers that were beautiful at the time that we purchased them. We would come home, dig up the ground, and plant them. We were very diligent in our efforts. They looked good for about a week, but then they would begin to wither and eventually die. This year, I decided to accept the help of a young man at my church, who volunteered to help me maintain our property and flowerbeds.

A few months ago, Mable and I took our annual trip to purchase flowers. The young man who was planning to help us suggested that we purchase some topsoil along with the new plants. We didn't pay much attention to his request and proceeded to purchase the flowers, completely forgetting the topsoil. Although he didn't say anything to me, we noticed that he was planting the seedlings in a soil that looked a little different than what was previously there. When I asked what it was, he said, "Topsoil that you already had in the garage."

I am delighted to report that it has been several months since we planted and the flowers are still going strong! What is even more significant is that the weather conditions during these months have not always been very favorable. Yet they are more than surviving; they are actually growing and thriving. There has not been more than a sprinkling of rain for these last three weeks. Temperatures have plummeted into the 30s and yet they still flourish. The only thing that has been different this year has been the "topsoil."

When contemplating marriage, you must look for an individual who has matured in the area of relationships and lives in a community rich in relational "topsoil" (healthy relationships). I refer to this as a community of Successful Support Systems (SSS). A community of Successful Support Systems produces Successful Spouses. In this chapter, you will learn how to identify persons who have been nurtured in the rich "topsoil" of successful relationships. You will only be a Successful Spouse to the degree that you have developed your relationship skills in a community of Successful Support Systems.

These SSS communities do actually exist. Maybe you have become disillusioned and have begun to think that the individualism and materialism we see all around us is the norm. One of the greatest challenges to those seeking marriage today is to find a healthy functioning marriage. It is almost impossible to find an acceptable model on television. One of the reasons *The Cosby Show* was so refreshing was that it gave us some hope that a marriage and, even more importantly, a healthy family can exist in this day and time. The reason *The Cosby Show* could be based on marriage and a healthy family is that its writer and producer—Dr. Bill Cosby—was a person who could wear the Successful Support System label well. He has been married for many years and has been very successful in raising his family.

When God created the world, He created vegetation, plants, and fruit with seed in it. His instruction to them was to reproduce "after its own kind." This initiated the law of reproduction, which governs all reproductive processes on planet earth. Everything reproduces "after its own kind." The good, the bad, the beautiful, the ugly, the admirable, and the deplorable all reproduce "after their own kind." Thus, in theory, unsuccessful marriages and successful marriages likewise produce "after their own kind." Haven't you noticed that military parents most often have children who join the military? Ministry parents produce ministry kids, and musically talented parents often produce musically gifted offspring. Likewise, the success or failure of a parent's marriage is repeated in the marriage of the children, which is why we continue to see the soaring divorce rate in America. Divorce is so common-place that it has become the model, mold, and norm for how 67% of marriages end. Thus, in theory, marriages ending in divorce are also reproducing "after their own kind."

On the international front, the institution of marriage is maintaining great success. In Japan, for example, the divorce rate is less than 1%, and the Japanese are disturbed by that statistic. When we survey most of the countries of the world, the institution of marriage is under the greatest threat in the United States (and in some, but not all, of the other western civilized nations).

If you peek into some of our ethnic communities, you will find marriages and families that are very much intact and flourishing. Marriages in these communities are strong and healthy, primarily because these groups have not allowed themselves to be polluted by our morally degenerating society. When the average American hears of the standards of courtship and marriage practiced in these cultures, they dub them as "old fashioned." However, you'll not only find that marriages and families in these cultures are thriving, you'll find a low rate of pre-marital pregnancy and divorce, as well.

Characteristics of a Successful Support System

What are the characteristics of an individual who has a Successful Support System? What do male and female "plants" look like that have been nurtured in the "topsoil" of a Successful Support System?

First, the woman will never be the pursuer of the man—not under any circumstances. She understands the negative impact it has on a man's attitude towards her when she assumes the role of hunter, rather than relinquishing this role to the man. Even though it is obvious to you (the female) that he is fond of you, he is taking a dreadfully long time to even ask you for your phone number. For most people, it would appear that he is dragging his feet. But you understand exactly what is going on. Both of you are clear on the procedure that is being followed. The procedure instructs those interested in each other not to get too close too soon. Rather, you observe character from a distance.

What are you looking for as you observe this person from a distance? You are looking for such qualities as truthfulness, trustworthiness, dependability, politeness, kindness, and integrity. These traits are not as immediately noticeable as superficial materialism, which normally catches the eye. But character will last when the new automobile and clothes have grown old and the pretty face starts to age. Remember the earlier definition that character is what you are when no one is watching or you don't think anyone is watching?

Second (and most importantly), you need to find out if that person is a growing, maturing Christian. Does that person faithfully attend a Bible Study and have an involvement in a ministry of the church? Is the person accountable to anyone?

When you're together, you should be treated like your sibling would treat you. It should be evident to you that this person understands that the Bible allows for only three possible relationships with those of the opposite sex:

1. Brother or Sister, which is inclusive of familial and spiritual brothers and sisters.
2. Engagement, which means pre-marital counseling classes have begun. It does not include persons with such contemporary designations as "my significant other."
3. Husband and Wife.

The fact that your companion treats you like a sister or brother is a clear indication that boundaries and restrictions are understood, which will limit the amount of one-on-one time the two of you spend together. Because your relationship is that of a brother

> *The fact that your companion treats you like a sister or brother is a clear indication that boundaries and restrictions are understood, which will limit the amount of one-on-one time the two of you spend together.*

and sister at this time, it is obvious that this person plans for a great deal of socialization and very little specialization. Specialization is defined as the time when you are only seeing and courting one person. It is for the engaged. It is not uncommon for this person to encourage going to the movies or bowling with a group rather than being on an exclusive date.

Third, each person is on guard not to say or do anything that would take the conversation or the relationship in the wrong direction. Their SSS have taught this individual how to avoid dangerous behaviors that befall dating couples, who ultimately wind up getting too close too soon. The typical dating couple ends up spending an inordinate amount of time with each other alone. There are late-night rendezvous and lengthy telephone conversations (which are more sexually probing than information gathering). These activities most often result in promiscuity and immorality. The consequences are immediate. This emotional and physical bonding hinders the couple's ability to candidly and objectively evaluate their relationship, as well as problems that may arise. Then, if marriage does occur, marital problems occur in the area of sexuality because they had sexual relations too soon. Since the couples become increasingly more obsessed with each other, they soon begin isolating themselves from family and friends. These are, in fact, the individuals that they so desperately need to help them properly evaluate the courtship. When you get too close too soon, it is so easy to become emotionally and physically involved. All too often, objectivity gives way to emotional chaos. A sane and sober evaluation of the relationship is surrendered.

Too often, it has been my experience that after counseling begins and serious issues and subjects are raised, it is obvious that these couples should postpone plans for marriage, or in some cases cancel it altogether.

A good example of this occurred at a workshop that Mable and I recently conducted. A young man began to discuss a particular dilemma that was causing him much concern. The woman he was planning to marry was a member of a church of another denomination. Specifically, he was Baptist and she was Catholic. The two Christian faiths have significantly different views on a variety of family and marital issues, as well as theological differences. For example, different views of infant baptism, different canonical teachings, and different books that make up the bible. Family matters include what birth control, if any, will be used and the education of the children. But, above all, where the family attends church on a regular basis is a major issue. This issue needs to be resolved before pre-marital counseling begins The young man was quite clear about the disasters that could ensue in their marriage from this problem.

When a husband and wife are worshipping at separate churches, there are several issues that can surface. Here are just a few of the problems that can arise: This might sound trite, but on Sunday mornings when they ought to be able to ride together in one car, they are again faced with the separation that occurs every other day of the week. More than likely, the wife will get in her car, the husband in his, and the family will go off in separate directions. An even larger problem that will result from not attending the same church is not having the benefit of sharing the same "spiritual diet" or eating from the same spiritual table. In other words, the husband and wife need to hear the same messages, participate in the same Bible studies, work side by side in ministry activities, and share in the same ministry fellowship groups. Perhaps the greatest problem that arises from this seemingly trivial issue involves the children. Which church will they attend? There are enough situations that divide a couple not to have the matter of which church they will attend bring added tension to the relationship.

I suggested to the young man several possible solutions, but he had already tried all of them. He was not prepared for the next answer I offered. It was simple, yet difficult. I suggested that perhaps they should not get married if this issue could not be resolved. It was obvious that this thought had actually crossed his mind. But undoubtedly he had decided not to act on what was clearly the best decision, primarily because they were engaged to be married. Knowing this fact, I can safely assume that he was emotionally, if not physically, involved with the young lady and, even more significantly, had socially and publicly obligated himself to marry her. He knew he was making a mistake and should not be contemplating marriage, but nonetheless, he was proceeding toward that end. This is a very dangerous scenario. I strongly suggest that pre-marital counseling take place before wedding plans are even discussed.

Moral Purity

Moral purity is much more than one might think. It's not just clean thoughts and right motives. The definition is comprised of four distinct areas.

1. Moral purity is more than abstinence. There are a lot of sexual activities
    you can engage in and be able to say you have not committed the
    actual act of sexual intimacy. There is telephone sex, masturbation,
    oral sex, and so on. Moral purity is more than being able to proclaim
    that you have not participated in the physical act of sex. We are setting
    the bar much higher. Because the problem of sexual immorality is so
    alarming, we must take drastic measures for a drastic problem.

    > *Dear friends, I urge you, as aliens and strangers in the world, to
    > abstain from sinful desires, which war against your soul.*
    > (1 Peter 2:11)

    Literally, this means to abstain from anything that arouses you
    sexually. This includes R—and X-rated movies, and many music
    videos that are filled with sex or sexual innuendos.

2. Moral purity places a strong emphasis on pure thoughts. We are
    to be very careful of our "thought life." Jesus' challenge to us in
    Matthew 6:27 is that if we look on a woman to lust after her body
    sexually, that is, imagining sex with her, we have already committed
    the sexual act in our heart. When you look at pornographic material,
    most of the time you are lusting after what is in the picture.

    > *To the pure, all things are pure, but to those who are corrupted and
    > do not believe, nothing is pure. In fact, both their minds and
    > consciences are corrupted.*
    > (Titus 1:15)

    > *Dear friends, this is now my second letter to you. I have written
    > both of them as reminders to stimulate you to wholesome thinking.*
    > (2 Peter 3:1)

    It has been proven that in the cities where there are "peep shows,"
    the incidence of rape is higher than in cities where it is not allowed.
    Thus, it is obvious that you can be stimulated to unwholesome
    and wholesome thinking.

3. Morally pure individuals flee sexual immorality.

Flee from sexual immorality. All other sins a man commits are
outside his body, but he who sins sexually, sins against his own body.
(1 Corinthians 6:18)

Is "dating" in its traditional form "fleeing sexual immorality?" I think not. When we put a young woman and a young man together in a car and tell them "Be careful; don't do anything sinful," we are really deceiving ourselves. Take another example: A woman dressed in a dress above her knees when she is standing up, or who is wearing a tight blouse in a room alone with a young man with hormones on top of his head, what do you expect them to do? The Bible says to "flee." Dating is not "fleeing."

On a trip home from college, my nephew, Khris, asked me, "What does the Bible have to say about dating?" Very quickly there was an inner response by the Holy Spirit that the Bible has nothing to say about dating because dating is not a biblical principle.

4. Morally pure individuals pursue sanctification and Godly character.

It is God's will that you should be sanctified: that you should avoid
sexual immorality; that each of you should learn to control his own
body in a way that is holy and honorable, not in passionate lust like
the heathen, who do not know God; and that in this matter no one
should wrong his brother or take advantage of him. The Lord will
punish men for all such sins, as we have already told you and warned
you. For God did not call us to be impure, but to live a holy life.
(1 Thessalonians 4:3-7)

What SSS Know

The next great benefit an individual derives from having been nurtured by SSS (that is, from those who have had success in maintaining healthy, long-lasting, and enduring relationships) is that they learn relationship skills. These individuals are at a distinct advantage over those who go into relationships with no training or understanding of what it takes for relationships to last. Most of our struggles with relationships are the result of the lack of some information about a given subject. ". . . my people are destroyed for a lack of knowledge." (Hosea 4:6) The following incident will help explain this point.

I will never forget an experience I had while visiting a church in which we had not previously ministered. I was curious about the church membership and their pastors and how we should attempt to minister to them. I asked a pastoral colleague and mutual friend in that same town what approach I should take. I tend to be a rather outgoing person who considers no one a stranger.

Further, I am accustomed to the host pastor picking us up, showing us the city, taking us out to eat, and so on. But I was warned that this would not be the case at this church. In fact, there would be very little, if any, contact with the pastor except at church. I was told that engaging in a lot of dialogue would be extremely offensive to our hosts. The church would provide us with the very best accommodations we had probably ever had, but that would be the extent of their hospitality. Additionally, we were cautioned not to be offended by this, but to understand that this was a part of the pastor's personality. The weekend went precisely as predicted. Several times I had to remind myself of the information I had been given. Because of what we were told, we made the necessary mental adjustments and got along quite well with our hosts—when we saw them.

As this story shows, the more information you receive before going into unfamiliar, unchartered waters, the better you are able to navigate and make it to your intended destination. It also helps when the person giving instructions and directions has had success getting there himself. The married or courting couple, who has been under the tutelage of SSS, will get to their destination without as much stress as those who are without the same kind of care. They will also be able to avoid bailing out and having to retrace their steps in relationships because they learned to trust the voice of their SSS.

Stages of a Courtship Process

What should impress you most about a person is his or her understanding of how the overall courtship process should evolve. Dr. Don Raunikar, in his book *Choosing God's Best*, offers a seven-stage Courtship Process.[2] The following are a few aspects of this process that are unique and helpful in building healthy relationships that will ultimately lead to marriage. The first three stages of his process would only be known to a well-trained SSS disciple.

Stage 1:

*   Identity in Christ

Most individuals in a dating situation assume that to begin a relationship that will culminate in marriage they should meet their "date" at a destined place. Then they move from there to a romantic dating relationship. I suggest that since those kinds of encounters typically lead to unsuccessful relational conclusions, that a better place to start a relationship is by developing a close kinship with Jesus Christ. As we have demonstrated, all healthy, growing, and vibrant relationships are built on a solid relationship with Jesus Christ.

Stage 2:

*   Ministry Involvement

Understand your purpose in life and begin "walking" in that purpose. This purpose should become your ministry. The truly fulfilled person in life is the one who is doing what he or she has been called and ordained to do from the "foundation of the world." Conversely, the most frustrated individual is the person who does not have a clue as to what direction his or her life should take. This is the person who bounces from job to job, changes majors three or four times in school, and is in and out of relationships. Run from that individual!

Why should Ministry Involvement be included in the Courtship Process? What better place to find someone who is Successfully Single and Successfully Serving than in ministry? Likewise, what better venue for observing someone's character from a distance than while you work with them on a ministry project?

Stage 3:

*   Foundation Building

It is at this stage that the potential spouse demonstrates spiritual, emotional, and relational commitments. When individuals in relationships can begin to understand the patterns of human behavior, most of their relationships will improve.

With respect to personalities, author Tim LaHaye's book *Spirit Controlled Temperament* has been the most beneficial resource for understanding the phenomenon that we call "human behavior." LaHaye helps us understand why we act the way we act and why those around us don't necessarily act the same way. He also helps us identify the strengths and weaknesses of our temperament. When we understand what our weaknesses are, we are able to begin praying for a particular fruit of the Spirit to provide balance in these particular areas.

Here are two perfect examples:

Mable and I have a wonderful relationship with a couple where the husband is a spontaneous person but the wife is a very scheduled individual. I know ahead of time that if I call and ask them to go out for a bite to eat tonight, her response will be, "Oh no, Pastor, I can't do that tonight!" I interpret what she has said in light of her temperament, knowing that what she is really saying is, "Oh no, Pastor, I have not planned that or put that in my schedule. I need more than a few hours notice to rearrange my life." What I've learned to do is to talk to her husband and let him do his thing. They will usually call back to say "All right."

Another example is a person in my family who has a confrontational temperament. If you challenge him, you are in for a good fight. I have learned to approach this individual differently. If you want to get a point across, back off and give him a little space. Then you can gently make your appeal. If I were not aware of this, there would be many wars at our family gatherings. Once you develop insight into human behavior, then you can anticipate the responses of those you're involved with. This skill will help you avoid being broadsided by unanticipated responses.

Appendix B to this book provides a snapshot of the information covered in each of the chapters. As you try to understand what your particular temperament type is, remember that you are really a blend of at least two temperaments. You have a predominant temperament and secondary one. So as you read the weaknesses and strengths of the various temperaments, you may see yourself in many of the particular types, while at the same time noticing that you are not like some of the characteristics listed. But you will probably recognize some of the characteristics of your primary temperament balanced by your secondary one.

Pay close attention to the weaknesses of your temperament blend. If you want to improve your quality of life, learn what your weaknesses are and try to work on them through the aid of the Holy Spirit. By the way, all of your friends and family know exactly what your weaknesses are, so you might as well own up to them.

Stage 4:

*   The Friendship Stage

The single person who has been trained by a SSS knows how to be a friend, which is the antithesis of "boy/girlfriend" and "significant other." There is no need to exaggerate and no need to pretend. We're just friends. What you see is what you get! You want to come over? The car is dirty . . . I'm having a real bad hair day—come over at your own risk. We're friends and there is no need for lies.

Single Adults who have been blessed in having a Successful Support System are clear about the correct reasons to get married. For those of you who are not clear, you should review the following list.

The Top 10 *Wrong* Reasons to Get Married

1. **We make such a lovely couple.** Beauty is in the eye of the beholder. If you ask someone else what they think of you, they might tell you that you make an ugly couple.
2. **I want to have guilt-free sex.** This is definitely the wrong reason. Married folks will tell you that they just don't have sexual intimacy every time they want it. It's not always appealing after a long day at work or after children arrive. There are the proverbial "headache" and "I'm too tired" scenarios more often than you think.

3. **He loves my children or I'm pregnant.** If you're pregnant and you get married because of the child, that child becomes the object of your scorn when you begin having problems (which, inevitably, you will) in the marriage. "If it weren't for you, I wouldn't be in this mess." Often people will advise you to do the "honorable thing," but pregnancy is not the right reason to get married. Not for the child OR the parents.

4. **We've been together so long, we really know each other and it's almost as if we're already married.** You're not! Statistics show that 85 percent of people who get married after living together get divorces.

5. **I need to get away from my parents.** "They're getting on my nerves! I've got to get out of this house." Independence is pulling at your mind. "I want to be able to do my own thing when I want to and without having to answer to anyone. I am more than capable of running my own life." You only "think" that you are. Besides, once you are married, you have to answer to your spouse.

6. **I'm tired of being alone.** You can be married and still be alone, living in the same house.

7. **He/She's got enough money to take care of me.** Money is not a cure for everything.

8. **It's time for me to settle down.** The thought here is because an individual has been "playing the field," the right thing to do is to settle down and get married. The problem with this rationale for marriage is that the individual most often has not divorced him or herself from a roving, unsettled spirit, which does not go away with a marriage mate. There really must be some space put between "playing the field" and settling down. Time needs to be given to "de-program" a roving mentality.

9. **He/She knows how to make me happy.** This certainly makes sense. Find someone to make me happy. But for the moment, you must accept that this is not a correct reason for marriage. Happiness is temporary—it's based on what's happening right now. Also, what makes you happy today may not make you happy next week.

10. **We're in love.** Every day, divorce courts across America are filled with couples who have been in love and often are still in love, but they just can't get along. Certainly, loving someone is a legitimate reason for marriage. But the question is how do we know this is really love (since we have felt this same way before). Many will testify that the person they once thought they were truly in love with now heads their list of despised persons. Jeremiah 17:9 says, "The heart is more deceitful than all else and is desperately sick; who can understand it?"

Unfortunately, all of these reasons for getting married are self-centered ones. With this attitude of self-centered appeasement, the marriage is bound to dissolve.

How Much SSS Involvement?

The model for Successful Support Systems finds its origin in Genesis 24. In that chapter, Abraham assigns his chief of staff, Eliezer, the task of finding a bride for his son Isaac. Today, he would be considered a matchmaker. This was the first level of involvement of a SSS in the successful marriage of Isaac and Rebekah.

When Eliezer found Rebekah at the town's well and told her of his intentions, he was immediately ushered into the presence of her family, the next level of a SSS. Rebekah's family scrutinized this man to find out things that might have escaped them under other circumstances. The scrutiny was warranted by their need to protect Rebekah and the fact that more than a man and a woman were getting married—actually two families were being joined together. Notice what Rebekah had obviously learned from her SSS. We see her participating in the daily chores. She is quite willing to serve a visitor to her small village, even giving his camels water. Rebekah was a Successful Servant.

She also had been taught that no matter how impressive the young man was (or in this case his father's servant), his first order of business was to meet with the family and receive their approval. But in this story, there is an un-named group of SSS. It is the community in which Rebekah lived. The community fostered the kind of culture and general attitude toward courtship that it expected of her—to behave in precisely the manner in which she did. It also prescribed for Eliezer the manner in which he would approach this lovely virtuous woman.

The person who has a SSS will have an "Eliezer" who will help identify the person he or she will marry. He or she will also have a cadre of family and friends who will scrutinize the intended person from top to bottom. This level of involvement will significantly contribute to a successful relationship.

This level of a Successful Support System will likely be a rare commodity for most readers of this book. In the community in which we live, the divorce rate is soaring and premarital habitation and pregnancy are "standard fare." Also, there are few accountability structures in place to which singles must submit.

You have to look long and hard to find a community that will support principles of moral purity, servant hood, and courtship rather than dating and submission to families. One of the few communities available to single adults is the "community of faith." There are churches that are offering this level of support for singles looking for proper nurturing and premarital oversight.

Let us encourage those of you who will become part of a Successful Support System. You will be a valuable commodity to those who are getting married. They desperately need your help. For the most part, those you will serve will more than likely fall into two potential marriage groups: those who have never been married (individuals who don't know what they are getting into) and those who are remarrying after a divorce (those who did not know what they were doing when they were first married). Remember, even though divorcees are getting married again, they may not have learned from their mistakes or gathered any essentials about how to do it right the next time around.

When George W. Bush was nominated as the Republican Party's presidential candidate, he went about the task of selecting a "running mate." The decision to make Dick Chaney his vice presidential running mate was not made by President Bush alone. He had the aid of a support team who had experience in this matter. It was a very important decision to make, since his election could have been jeopardized by the wrong choice. It is imperative that the vice president complements the personality and politics of the president. If the president of the United States needs help selecting someone to serve with him for four years—or at best, eight years—surely one needs help to find a suitable "running mate" to serve in partnership for a lifetime. What I am suggesting is that one of the main functions of a Successful Support System is to help in the selection of a mate.

CHAPTER 6

Successful Sailing

Here's a bit of practical advice for those of you who are looking for a spouse (and this might sound a bit strange): don't look too hard. Don't make looking a preoccupation, and definitely don't put more effort into your search than your effort to cultivate a relationship with God (Matthew 6:33).

Some preachers love to play golf, some love to travel—I love to shop. But what I find most interesting is that I usually get my best bargains when I am not looking for anything in particular! These are times when I'm just perusing stores and looking to see what's out there. The same is true regarding mate selection—the best way to find one is not to be so serious about it. Most great marriages often began by each spouse simply being at the right place at the right time doing the right thing.

> Be assured that God is aware of your stage in life and He is capable of advancing your cause when it is the right time.

Desperation has caused countless individuals to accept less than God's best. In their desperation, they confused God's voice with the voice of their impatience and emotion. This has resulted in failed relationships and divorce. Be assured that God is aware of your stage in life and He is capable of advancing your cause when it is the right time.

You really can go to heaven without a spouse. Don't look so hard. Don't be obsessed with it—marriage is not the cure-all for your problems. How often do you hear (or say), "If I can just get married . . . ." But, in all reality, it doesn't matter—if you are mean, can't handle your money, don't enjoy talking with people, undisciplined, or don't have a good job or education, you will still be all these things after you are married. Marriage is not the cure-all for solving all the inequities in your life.

If you are contented in your singleness (successfully serving and submitting with successful support systems in place) and you are ready for the journey of marriage, you must remember to take seven "essentials" with you as you make the trek. They will assure you safe travels on the trip of becoming a "Successful Spouse."

Essential 1:

Know Who You Are in Christ.

If you don't know who you are in Christ and you get married, you are going to make a mess of things. You'll be married, but you'll have poor relations with your wife, children, and others in the community. You need to know that you are God's child. You are not a child of the devil or a child of the world. You are a child of God. Knowing who you are in Christ (the righteousness of God and a new creature who is fearfully and wonderfully made) and operating in your purpose will make life so much easier and fulfilling for you.

Learn to please God. Seek to please God. I Corinthians 7:32 says the aim of the person who is single should be to please the Lord. That's essential. You know you are a child of God if you have accepted Jesus Christ as your personal Lord and Savior. As a single Christian, He has given each of you a gift that is uniquely yours—the gift of singleness.

In I Corinthians 7, Paul says one person has one gift, another has another gift. God loves you and you are His child. You need to know that God has given you the gift of singleness right now in your life. If He didn't love you, He'd give you the gift of marriage in your life before you were ready for it. (And there are a whole lot of folks who got married before they were ready for it.) But God says: not for you—I have given you the gift of singleness. Every good and perfect gift comes down from above. You think she's gorgeous and you think she'd be the perfect gift for you. You think he's handsome— "Lord, my life would be just right." The marriage would be a gift, just not a good gift or a perfect gift. The reason you know God loves you is because He's making you wait a little while. Don't go on the trip of life without this essential: know who you are in Christ.

Essential 2:

Have A Positive Self-Image.

Live a life where you are pleased with who you are and what you stand for. Learn how to love yourself. Learning to love yourself means seeing yourself as Jesus does, accepting yourself, and respecting yourself. Some of you readers need to work on your poor self-image. Here is a practical place to use what you have learned from your new study of the temperaments. Every temperament has strengths and weaknesses. Focusing and dwelling on those weaknesses is debilitating. It depresses you and saps you of your mental and physical strength. Likewise, each temperament has its strengths. When our strengths are fueled by the power of the Holy Spirit of God within us, we become energized and empowered. As the scripture in Philippians 4:13 states, "I can do all things through Christ . . . ." When you are walking in your strengths and not your weaknesses, competent achievements begin to be a frequent visitor. Success has a wonderful way of increasing our self-confidence and building a very positive self image. For example, when I began gaining weight, my quality of life began to decrease. As a result of these factors, I was not happy with myself or my physical condition. When I got dressed, bulges and love handles were taking my positive self image on a downward spiral. But when I took control of my eating habits and began exercising and getting rid of the stress, I began to feel great about myself. Make every effort to control your weight by a disciplined diet of food, exercise, and rest. Your physical health is a strong contributor to a positive self-image.

Certainly at the top of the list of steps toward a more positive self image is living a life that is pleasing to God. Knowing God is pleased with your life allows you to feel good about yourself.

Take advantage of your season of singleness to fix a poor self-image. "Thou shall love thy neighbor as thyself" . . . in the manner that you love yourself. Some of you are not ready for marriage because of the way you love yourself. In fact, you don't really love yourself. Psalm 139:14 says "Lord, I praise you because I am fearfully and wonderfully made." The reason that so many people are mean and hateful and walk around with a chip on their shoulders is because they don't love, or even like themselves. It doesn't matter if you wear a size 24, you grew up without a father, didn't go to college, or have bad skin. God says that you are wonderful. Who says that a size 6 is the standard? Who said your birth was a mistake? Who said that? Where did that come from? It's a lie from the pit of Hell because God says you are fearfully and wonderfully made. Straighten your shoulders right now and tell yourself that you are wonderful. God made you and God never makes a mistake. God always knows what he is doing. He designed you in his image.

> *God always knows what he is doing. He designed you in his image.*

Essential 3:

Learn How to Handle Finances.

The third essential to take with you on this trip is how to handle finances according to God's design and plan. I Tim. 6:6-9 tells us that the love of money is the root of all evil; it does not say that money is the root of all evil. Some people have loved it and chased after it; because of that they have left the faith and gotten mixed up in a whole lot of hurtful things. Read the scripture for yourself. Be careful about chasing after money. Learn how to handle your finances. Learn how to save some money.

In fact, learn how to invest your money. If I were to try to advise you about how to invest your money, I could be charged with the felonious crime of violating interstate trade laws. However, what has worked well for many people in America has been investing in real estate. Generally speaking, the housing market has proven to be a great place to invest money even when other investment vehicles are not fairing well.

There is a general rule of thumb for successful money management—spend 70 percent, save 20 percent, and give God 10 percent. This is a good place to start if you want to become financially solvent.

In his newest work, *The Purpose Driven Life*, Rick Warren makes a challenging affront to the ever increasing indulgence of frivolously spending and wasting money. He writes:

Most people fail to realize that money is both a test and a trust from God. God uses finances to teach us to trust him, and for many people, money is the greatest test of all. God watches how we use money to test how trustworthy we are. The Bible says, "If you are untrustworthy about worldly wealth, who will trust you with the true riches of Heaven?"

This is a very important truth. God says there is a direct relationship between how I use my money and the quality of my spiritual life. How I manage my money ("worldly wealth") determines how much God can trust me with spiritual blessings ("true riches"). How do you fair in regard to your spending habits?[23]

Lastly, learn how to give God what you owe Him; you owe Him your tithes. You're not giving God your money when you pay your tithes. God says 10 percent is His. Read Malachi chapter three. He says if you don't give your tithes, you are cursed with a curse and when God curses you, no one can take the curse off of you. You can try to go to a palm reader or fortune teller to try to get the curse off, but when God curses you, you're cursed. But don't stop at the 10 percent, because when you pay your tithes, you're just demonstrating to God that you are honest. You haven't done anything special. If you want God to bless you, you have to demonstrate that you trust Him. That's what happens when you give an offering. When you pay tithes you're just demonstrating honesty; but when you give an offering, you're demonstrating your trust. You don't have to pray about whether or not you should tithe. Are you expecting God to change His word? You don't need to pray about it . . . just do it.

You don't need faith to tithe—you need honesty. Do you need faith to pay your car loan? Do you need faith to pay your rent or your mortgage? No, you just write the check; it's not your money. You need faith to give an offering. He says if you pay your tithes and give an offering, then He'll open up the windows of heaven. Don't expect the window to open just by paying your tithes. Some of you have been wondering why the windows haven't been opening. God said if you pay your tithes and offering, "I will open up the window of heaven and pour you out a blessing."

Successfully Singles' Financial Checklist

- ✓ Do you tithe regularly?
- ✓ Do you give an offering regularly?
- ✓ Do you save regularly?
- ✓ Do you have a checking account?
- ✓ Do you pay for most items with cash or a debit card?
- ✓ Do you pay your bills on time?
- ✓ Do you have a budget?
- ✓ Do you have any money invested?

Essential 4:

Learn How to Submit.

Learn to deal with submission before you get married. A good place for you to start is by practicing submission on your job. Do not disrespect and undermine your employer; learn to submit. Practice submission in your family relationships. Brothers, submit to your sisters; sisters, submit to your brothers; children, to your parents; parents, to your children. Practice submitting so that when you get married it won't be a new concept. Ephesians 5:21 says to submit yourselves one to another. Husbands and wives have to submit, children also have to submit. Parents, there is a whole lot of submitting that's got to go on in your life. The quicker you learn this, the better off you'll be and the better example you'll be for your children.

My Aunt Catherine once asked, "Do you know that freedom is dangerous?" You must learn how to handle freedom because if you get too much, it will ruin you. So many young people want to leave home early to get out from under their parental authority. I left, but was I ever glad to get back! Get a hold of this submission principle; don't leave home without it. Don't start on this trip without it.

Essential 5:

Learn How to Communicate.

James 1:19 says we ought to be quick to listen, slow to speak, and slow to become angry. Would you consider yourself a good listener? Ask someone who is close to you. Do you think or, for that matter, even pause before you speak? It doesn't take much for some of you to get angry. All it takes is for someone to look at you the wrong way and you become agitated or confrontational. Learn how to communicate; be slow to speak. Can you practice listening just a little bit? Be slow to speak and quick to listen.

The first thing you need to do when you're having a conversation is seek to understand what the person is saying. I know you want to let them know what you are thinking, but it should not be that way. You frequently say: "Listen, just hear me first. You don't ever try to listen to me, wait; just hear me out." The thing you should do is to seek first to understand. You've got to learn how to communicate. "But the tongue can no man tame, it is an unruly evil, full of deadly poison" (James 3:10). You can kill somebody with your tongue. You don't have to lay a hand on them. You can wound their spirit so that they never recover in life.

Women, please understand that when you are arguing, you normally have the verbal advantage. The typical man can not keep up with you in an argument. You can go up one side of us and down the other. When you get through killing us with your tongue, we feel like we are about one foot tall. Men who don't have the Holy Spirit don't know how to handle this kind of abuse. The only recourse they feel they have is to use their physical strength to their advantage, WHICH IS WRONG! Women, learn how to control your tongue and learn how to communicate in a quiet and gentle manner.

> *Do not let any unwholesome talk come out of your mouths but only what is helpful for building others up according to their needs, that it may benefit those who listen.*

> (Ephesians 4:29)

Know that when you are criticizing, lying, and berating others, it is sin. And the "wages of sin is death."

In that same regard, men need to learn to control their tongues. But more often, they need to learn to use them with greater frequency. According to my wife Mable, if men really plan to live with a woman for the rest of their lives in the holy state of matrimony, it would behoove them to learn the art of talking to a woman.

In his book *His Needs-Her Needs: Building an Affair-Proof Marriage*, Willard Harley, Jr. shares with us the results of a survey.[4] The purpose of this survey was to find out what the emotional needs of men and women are and how each would rank those needs in order of priority. The results indicated that the preponderance of the women surveyed felt that communication is second in order of importance to them, only to be surpassed by their need for affection. Harley further verifies what most women already knew, that when a wife has an extra-marital affair, it is not because she wanted a sexual fling (even though that may well be the inevitable result), but because she desired an authentic, uninterrupted dialogue with someone who says they love her. The record will show that her husband had stopped fulfilling that need and left her vulnerable in the area of communication. After over thirty years of marriage, I have come to understand that most often men talk to make a point, whereas women talk to get close. The man that will win, and continue to woo his lifetime companion, is the man who has developed his communication skills to the degree that his mate loves talking and communicating with him.

Essential 6:

Develop a Forgiving Spirit.

The Lord's Prayer says, "Forgive us our trespasses as we forgive those who trespass against us." Then later, Jesus says, "If you forgive not men their trespasses, neither will your heavenly Father forgive you your trespasses." It is a dangerous thing for a Christian not to forgive someone. What you are really saying is, "Lord I'm not going to forgive them and I'm giving you permission now not to forgive me." This means you better not ever mess up; you better not ever do anything else wrong. And guess what? You are going to do something wrong. But Ephesians 4:32 says: "Be kind and compassionate one to another, forgiving each other just as in Christ God has forgiven you." Just as God has forgiven you for all your sins, you've got to forgive. Not just sins you commit, but things that you omit to do. He that knoweth to do good and doeth it not, to Him it is sin.

In summary, put God in all your plans; put Him in everything you do. In all your ways, acknowledge Him and He will direct you around life's difficulties (Proverbs 3:5-7). He'll direct you away from a bad relationship that you were just about to get into. He'll guard your heart. If you trust Him, He'll work it out. In all your ways, acknowledge Him. If He leads you, you'll always walk right. You will have mastered the art of Successful Sailing.

Sailing . . .

It's Wednesday night. Mable and I are headed to Ocean City to spend a week in a beach condo. Since there is no schedule or time restraints involved, we are going to drive the two hour trip relaxed and unstressed. There is no need to rush.

"TL, what time would you like to leave tomorrow?" asked Mable.

"Let's shoot for noon," I responded.

Thursday morning, 12 noon.
"Mable, are you ready?"

"Not yet" comes the expected reply.

"How much longer will you be?" I cautiously inquired."

"Another ten minutes or so," Mable responded.

I am quite aware that the response given really means, "I don't know right now."

"Mable, I thought you were ready. I just took your suitcase down stairs; what else do you have to pack?

"I'm packed, it's just all that other stuff," came the reply.

The night before, I fell asleep while she was still getting things together for our trip. When I awoke, I saw Mable's suitcase packed and closed and thought, "Wow, we are going to be able to get to leave at our scheduled time today, she is ready to go." I forgot that a packed bag does not necessarily mean "ready to leave." What it does indicate is that the dresses, blouses, skirts, and shoes have been prepared for travel in the suitcase. But what's left are the small, incidental items that do not go into the suitcase. For instance, there are books, a church phone directory, an iron, Planet Solution (for bathing), sun lotion, sun block, and so on.

"Have I gotten everything?" Mable asks.

"Yep," I said, without giving it a thought.

When we drive we love to take goodies from the kitchen. In other words, although we may have completed the general packing of clothes and other items, there is still some final packing to do. I retrieved the cooler from the garage and filled it with ice. The night before, while I was asleep, Mable decided to surprise me with one of my favorite snacking foods, her award-winning Tuna Salad. That goes into the cooler, while bottled water, juices, and assorted fruit take up the space that's left.

It is 1:15 p.m. We are still at home, but it's alright because even though we missed our deadline for departure, we are going to be well prepared for the trip. We are well equipped with all the accoutrements, which make for an exceptional drive and vacation (most of which would have been left behind if we were in a rush to arrive at our destination). Now what is noteworthy is that none of these items would have stopped us from making the trip. We would never have turned around to retrieve the bottled water or juice, but having them makes the trip much more enjoyable. In fact, we could have stopped along the way or waited until we arrived to purchase the items. But because we left home with these items in our possession, the trip. We were finally all packed and ready for a wonderful trip. Do you notice any similarities in preparing for a lifetime marriage trip?

In closing, I am compelled to tell one last story (about another trip Mable and I took together). The two of us had been on many vacations together in our more than thirty years of marriage. But about five years ago, we embarked on our first cruise ship vacation. Others had tried to prepare us for the vacation by telling us of the joys that awaited us, but we were really not getting the full picture. There are some things that you just cannot explain. Now, after the wonderful time we experienced, we are trying to explain it to others. The same is true of marriage! The joys of marriage really cannot be explained—they must be experienced. To many, it is the ultimate life experience. Sure there are those beginning years when it's just the two of you frolicking together without the interruptions of anyone else in the house. And then the children show up and present another set of joys and pleasures (school plays, football games, and Christmases).

As with the cruise ship, everything that is enjoyable, pleasurable, and memorable is included in the trip! You do not have to leave the ship for anything (not to mention the fact that if you tried to leave the ship while it was in route, it would be detrimental to your health!). One of the greatest joys that can be experienced in marriage is the experience of working together in business or ministry. Mable and I are blessed to work together in ministry, even in the writing of this book. It is a delight to have someone who shares your goals, dreams, and aspirations working with you side-by-side. But let's not forget the retirement years, which, if truth be told, are really the best years. I refer to those years as "life on cruise control." A little money saved; plenty of time on your hands. The best way to say it is when you are married to the right person, life gets better and better. It's a long journey, but when you have properly *prepared* and have been properly *paired* with the right person, there is no experience on earth that can really compare to the joy that the union brings.

Have there been successes in the Successful Souse Selection process? Many! I must tell you that this can be done. There are dozens of couples who were successfully single, successfully served, successfully submitted, and are now sailing while enjoying the sweetness of life in Christ Jesus with a perfect mate.

ENDNOTES

[1]   Raunikar, D., "A Prescription for Failure," in *Choosing God's Best: Wisdom for Lifelong Romance*, pp. 33-54, Sisters, Oregon: Multnomah Publishers, Inc., 1998.

[2]   Raunikar, D., "Making a 'Good' Choice or a 'God' Choice," in *Choosing God's Best: Wisdom for Lifelong Romance*, pp. 75-128, Sisters, Oregon: Multnomah Publishers, Inc., 1998.

[3]   Warren, R., *The Purpose Driven Life: What on Earth Am I Here For?* p. 46, Grand Rapids, Michigan: Zondervan, 2002.

[4]   Harley, W., *His Needs-Her Needs: Building an Affair-Proof Marriage,* Willard Harley, Jr. Grand Rapids, Michigan: Fleming H. Revell Company, Baker House, 2001.

APPENDIX A

Characteristics of the unaccountable:

- They have a loose spirit with few boundaries.
- They often try to rationalize and justify why they do the things they do.
- They make decisions without consulting other people. Isn't it interesting that some folks come to you after they've made the decision to tell you what they will do and solicit a blessing on what they've already decided? That's not accountability. Being accountable is seeking prayer before you make the decision.
- They are detached or reclusive, isolated from people. Be careful about getting involved in a relationship when the individual no longer wants you to be around your family and friends.
- There is a lack of authenticity and realness about them. They are fake and lie continuously. You can never trust anything that they say.
- They are defensive.
- They are unwilling to admit to mistakes and failure.
- They hide major areas of their lives from others. For example, they might make comments such as:

  > "Well, that's something I don't talk about."
  > "You don't need to know about that."
  > "I don't talk about my family stuff."
  > "I don't talk about the kind of work I do."
  > "That's none of your business."

Do you know anybody like that?
- They are intimidating, unapproachable, and very secretive. You can never approach them with anything. They always have a chip on their shoulder. If you say the least little thing, they get very defensive.

- They are always confronting others. Do you know folks who are like that? Accountability and submission have to do with protection, so this type of person will neither be accountable or submissive to you.

Source: Adapted with permission from D. and B. Rainey, *Moments Together for Couples*, September 12 entry © 1995, Regal Books, Ventura, California, 93003.

APPENDIX B

The Four Temperaments

SANGUINE

Sanguines are warm, buoyant, lively and fun-loving people who are receptive by nature. External impressions easily find their way into their hearts and, as a result, they react readily by way of spontaneous response. They make decisions through feelings rather than reflective thought. Because they are super extroverts, Sanguines are usually the life of the party. They are seldom lost for words and, consequently, sometimes speak without thinking. They usually do not like to be alone.

Never lacking for friends, the Sanguine's naive, impulsive and congenial nature opens doors and hearts to them. Their noisy, blustery, friendly ways make them appear more confident than they really are, while their energetic and lovable disposition gets them through the rough spots of life.

Strengths	Weaknesses
Warm emotions	Undisciplined
Friendly	Weak-willed
Fun-loving	Egotistical
Outgoing/extrovertish	Emotionally excitable
Enthusiastic	Unstable
Talkative	Prone to exaggerate
Responsive	Disorganized
Compassionate	Hot-tempered
Stimulating	Manipulative
Ambitious	Restless

CHOLERIC

Cholerics are the hot-quick, active, practical, strong-willed, temperamental type who are self-sufficient and very independent. They tend to be decisive and opinionated; therefore, they find it easy to make decisions both for themselves and for others. They can be extroverts, but not to the degree of the Sanguine. They thrive on activity and do not need the environment to stimulate them because they stimulate the environment. Cholerics rarely do anything "just for nothing" because there is an underlying reason for everything they do.

They are not frightened by adversity but rather encouraged by it. Cholerics are determined to succeed where others have failed. They are strong natural leaders. They do not sympathize easily with others and do not show their emotions readily. Cholerics are often embarrassed or disgusted by their tears, so they may become insensitive to the needs of others.

Strengths	*Weaknesses*
Strong-willed	Unemotional and cold
Determined	Self-sufficient
Independent	Impetuous
Decisive	Domineering
Active and energetic	Unforgiving
Practical	Hostile and volatile
Strong natural leader	Sarcastic and cruel
Optimistic/confident	Impatient
Productive	Unsympathetic
Goal-oriented	Opinionated

MELANCHOLY

This is the richest of all the temperaments. Melancholy personalities are the analytical, self-sacrificing, gifted, perfectionist types with a very sensitive emotional nature. They lean toward the fine arts and often appear moody. They don't make friends easily but, when they do, they are good faithful friends. They are reluctant to take people at face value, so they are prone to be suspicious of others.

This is also the most pessimistic of the temperaments, although they will tell you that they are being realistic, not negative. They sometimes display some moods where they produce great work, but often this is followed by bouts of deep depression.

They find their greatest joy through self-sacrifice. They enjoy making themselves suffer and often choose very hard tasks for their vocations. Once they get the hang of their work, they are usually good at what they have chosen to do. Their mind is both their strength and their weakness. They have wide mood swings—high highs and low lows. They will withdraw. Because they are task-oriented rather than relationship-oriented, they may rebel against authority.

Strengths	*Weaknesses*
Gifted	Moody
Analytical	Deeply emotional
Perfectionist	Easily offended
Self-disciplined	Pessimistic
Industrious	Negative
Self-sacrificing	Critical and picky
Aesthetic	Theoretical/impractical
Creative	Suspicious/revengeful
Loyal and faithful	Self-centered

PHLEGMATIC

These are the calm, easy-going, never-get-upset individuals with such high boiling points that they seldom become angry. Phlegmatics are the most likable of all the temperaments. Life for them is mellow and pleasant. It is an experience in which they avoid as much involvement as possible. They often feel more than they are willing to admit. They attract friends because they enjoy people and have a natural, dry sense of humor. They have a positive approach to life. Although they are very hard to motivate, Phlegmatics can produce very well once they are motivated. They prefer the day-to-day routine. They often act like Christians even if they are not saved. They are not perfect, but appear to be more polite and diplomatic.

Strengths	Weaknesses
Calm	Passive and unmotivated
Cool	Procrastinating
Easy-going	Indecisive
Diplomatic	Fearful /filled with worry
Dependable	Unsure
Orderly	Self-protective
Practical	Stubborn
Humorous	Selfish and stingy
Agreeable	Slow and lazy

Source: Data from T. LaHaye, *Spirit-Controlled Temperament*, pp. 65-72 and 75-88, ©
1992, Tim LaHaye, Tyndale House Publishers, Inc.